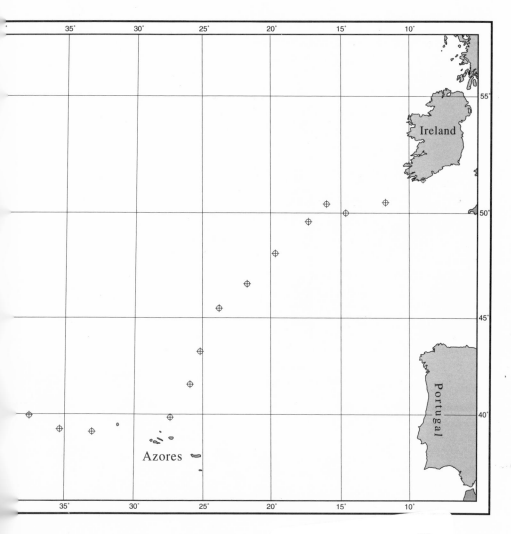

Ireland

Portugal

Azores

OUTBOUND

Clarity
Designer and Builder David M. Stainton and Associates
P.O. Box 129
Great Cranberry Island, Maine 04625
Length on deck 32 ft. 6 in.
Length waterline 26 ft. 10 in.
Beam 10 ft.
Draft 5 ft.
Sail area 540 sq. ft.

OUTBOUND

*Finding a Man
Sailing an Ocean*

WILLIAM STORANDT

The University of Wisconsin Press

THE UNIVERSITY OF WISCONSIN PRESS

1930 Monroe Street

Madison, Wisconsin 53711

www.wisc.edu/wisconsinpress

3 Henrietta Street

London WC2E 8LU, England

1   3   5   4   2

Printed in the United States of America

Library of Congress Cataloging-in-Publication Data

Storandt, William.
Outbound : finding a man, sailing an ocean /
William Storandt.
pp.   cm. — (Living out)
ISBN 0-299-17460-3 (alk.: cloth)
1. Storandt, William. 2. Gay men—Biography.
3. Homosexuality, Male. 4. Voyages and travels.
I. Title: Finding a man, sailing an ocean.
II. Title. III. Series.
HQ75.8.S76 A3   2001
306.76′6′092—dc21   2001000714

For Brian,

who always knew we would make it.

I'd like to thank Ellen James and Rob Lair for the acute eyes and ears they brought to their reading of this manuscript, and for the hundreds of improvements they suggested. I'd like to thank Diane Cleaver for her vision of what this work could be and for encouraging me to tell the whole story.

OUTBOUND

1

It's a hot, still, weekday dawn in the boatyard—nobody around, random gull squawks, the hum of the highway bridge. Brian, Bob, and I haul the dinghy aboard and lash it upside down on the foredeck. Bob heads for the washroom for a last shower; Brian works on the breakfast dishes. In a few minutes we will slip away to sail across the Atlantic Ocean. I scrub the slime off the dinghy bottom.

Just now we're waiting for Diana, our neighbor and close friend, who didn't expect or want to see us off. Bob, who never misplaces anything, has forgotten his wallet; Diana's been roused from bed to find it and bring it. There has been, in her attitude toward the whole venture, an undercurrent of "How could you put me through this worry?" She threw the bon voyage party, but then made it clear that she wanted nothing further to do with our departure.

I am outwardly wooden, going about last chores. Inside me a lopsided struggle is all but over. The part of me that's a sensible man in his forties is gagged in a gunnysack; the part that has tended the flame of this dream for the last twenty years is muscling me through the motions of departure. I'm the skipper—the fount of morale. But for the moment, a wooden outside is the best I can make of the ruckus inside. Brian, on the other hand, is fully on board, all for making it work, lost in getting all the egg yolk off the fork tines.

I stand on the dock, looking at *Clarity*. She sits dead motionless, gleaming, a thirty-three-foot dark green pod full of frozen casseroles, canned hams, and cookies. Her varnish catches the early sun. The last weeks of lists and sweat have made her ready.

Diana arrives, hair still pillow-squashed. Bob is braced for some ribbing, but she is serious, too sleepy to act upbeat. There are just perfunctory hugs.

This is it. Start the diesel, use up the first drop of fuel reserves. Record the distance log reading: 2157.03 miles. I am methodical, fearing to overlook something in my agitation. Diana hands us the dock lines one by one, her face lined with concern.

Clarity. The final weeks of lists and sweat have made her ready.

We back slowly out of the slip. *Clarity*'s keel has been sinking into the mud each low tide, so we're leaving at high tide. Stuck at the dock would be an omen. We will ride the ebb out to sea for the first six hours. It makes no difference what time you leave to sail thirty-five hundred miles, but I've got it in my head we must be out of sight of land by dark. A last look back: Diana waves, nervously rubbing her head with the other hand. In recent weeks some friends have withdrawn in a sulk of abandonment, others have burst into getting-things-said deathbed sort of talk. Only one or two have asked what they could do to help. The Connecticut River railroad bridge stands open. It closes just after we go through.

The cockpit and decks are tracked with boatyard mud, littered with dock lines, fenders, and my two buckets of fresh water. Brian humors me on this. We will trip over these until one tips over, maybe get one dinner's dish-rinsing out of the other, all in order to hoard the three tankfuls and six jerry-jugfuls a few extra hours.

The cameras are out. Bob snaps us, the intrepid couple, and then we do a self-timer shot of all three of us. Brian—lanky, black-haired, handsome even though still a bit office-pale—wears an excited, determined smile, entirely appropriate; my bring-on-the-adventure face is bogus; Bob—his full

Setting off from Saybrook, Connecticut, me, Brian, and Bob (left to right). Brian's excited, determined smile is entirely appropriate. My bring-on-the-adventure face is bogus. Bob looks game, but a bit as though he suspects a trick.

head of white hair carefully combed, almost croonerish, a held smile—looks game, but a bit as though he suspects a trick.

Fishermen pass us, headed after bluefish in Plum Gut. They've probably packed a couple of sandwiches, beers on the ice. If they knew where we were headed. We exchange tolerant waves. The sensible, shanghaied part of me envies them.

Across Long Island Sound, through the rapids of Plum Gut and we start across toward the south point of Long Island's swallowtail: Montauk, the last land. Brian is tidying up below, cut off by the clatter of the diesel. I don't even have to see him to know the jiggering intensity aimed at every spot on the counter. Bob and I stand on the cockpit seats. We've barely sailed with him at all. We decided a third crew member would make the passage less exhausting and therefore safer; the pool of people we knew with the time and inclination to join us totaled one: Bob. Steering with my ankle against the tiller, I manage a jaunty monologue in which I speak with quiet courage of my fears, implicitly dismissing them as inevitable, merely signs of sanity, warnings from a fainthearted side that must be mastered. Maybe

Bob buys it. He keeps up a good front, claiming he feels so lucky to be setting out on such an adventure, grinning about how this is all new to him. Can't mean it. Who is this guy, anyway? He suddenly seems too much a stranger—Diana's friend really—to be bound to us for this. I'm both burdened by the duty to act plucky for him and miffed that he doesn't seem to need my help.

It's still calm, hazy. The forecast is good. I'm pleased to be feeling well. Normally I'm never seasick, but the first time Brian and I headed off on an ocean passage, seven years ago in 1981, the weather and forecast were perfect, and I spent the first two days hanging over the side. I could see no omens in that weather either, but four days out commenced a three-day Force 10 storm that my parents saw on television. That time I was nervous setting out because it was the first time. This time I'm nervous because of that time. So far the pill is working.

Montauk is not appearing out of the haze. As long as we don't ram it, it makes no difference if we never see it, but still, it was to be the last sight of land. We've got a brand-new Loran receiver to tell us exactly where we are, and I turned it on as we were leaving so it has had plenty of time to "settle in." I'll just ask it where Montauk is. Acting as if I just can't decide which toy to play with next, I go below to the chart table to poke at the Loran's keypad membrane. Bad news: the latitude-longitude display is flashing. The instrument is saying Don't believe me, I'm lost too. My stomach does its first flip-flop. I didn't buy this instrument for the passage; it picks up limited-range transmitters arrayed along the coast and is not intended for offshore position finding. But we're still near the coast, well within range. How about if everything would just please work?

The distance log will at least help locate us. Offhandedly, I ask Brian to give me a log reading. 2157.03. The log is not working either. This is getting to the omen stage. Not dangerous—Columbus reckoned his position by throwing a wood chip off the bow and measuring how long it took to sail past it—but ominous. Brian sets to work on the log.

Whenever Murphy strikes, Brian and I have clear roles: I stew, he acts. Once in Baltimore after a night on the town, we returned to the dinghy to find it had drifted under the dock and was pinned there by the rising tide. It was Brian who dove into the midnight harbor, scrambled into the dinghy, and forced it out under the timbers. Another time, while leaving Trinidad at night through one of the channels known as the Mouths of the Dragon, we were becalmed in steep incoming swell with rock cliffs on either side and the diesel starter dead. It was Brian who jumped in the dinghy and, in a blur of oars, towed us out to the clear air. While I'm using mind control, attempting to undo the calamity by rewinding reality, Brian simply solves it. While I'm longing for other paths in life, free of whatever glitch we're facing, he's saying Right, this is the path and next up is to fix this glitch. This same resolve of his to see things through lets me weather our shoreside storms, feeling firmly chosen.

I look again at the Loran. It has stopped flashing: a true reading. Is this thing toying with me? I do not tell anyone about this. Because I did the installation? Nothing so petty. Without ever speaking about it, we each know that morale is to be coddled—no bad news, small gripes, or misgivings, unless absolutely necessary. For a worry wart this amounts to a vow of silence. I assume my self-possessed manner will appear serene.

In the late morning, a light breeze comes up. We hoist the biggest sails: full main and 150 percent genny. Too much sail perhaps, but we're eager to rack up the miles and, more important, to start off with the attitude that we will run the boat energetically—change sail whenever necessary, make the mint sauce with the lamb, change the pillowcases, hell, USE the pillowcases. What else is there to do? It is good to switch off the diesel, to feel *Clarity* heel and easily exceed her motoring speed, bearing onward her sacred cargo of water, long books, and Brooklyn deli kielbasy, using up no more of her sacred cargo of fuel. With the dinghy on deck rather than splatting along behind on its towrope the way it does when we're out for the day, our progress is eerily silent.

We're making hourly log entries of our compass course and estimated speed. As long as all the electronic gear is iffy, we'll have to add up these entries once a day for total distance run in order to do a position fix, the same as they did back before electrons were press-ganged onto boats, back when so many people died at sea. These fixes comprise what's known morbidly enough as the dead-reckoning track, which, when combined in an arcane recipe with our sextant sights of the sun, will produce a row of circled crosses advancing across the chart of the North Atlantic.

The yellow haze imperceptibly thickens to cloud cover, then to a dank mid-afternoon dusk. The wind builds steadily, we reduce sail in stages, switching to the one hundred percent jib, and lowering the mainsail part way to the first reef point, then the second, then the third, which leaves it as small as we can make it. We're tearing along at hull speed, heeled over as though we are sprinting to a finish line. I feel like a recovering alcoholic who has impulsively downed a pint of gin. I've betrayed myself; I'm bewildered that I could have let a bunch of harmless bluster, cocktail party conversation, come to pass as this appalling commitment to unspeakable discomfort and unthinkable danger.

We're maybe fifty miles out; I can just barely pick up *All Things Considered* from National Public Radio. This shortens by one day one of the deprivations we are entering upon. But rushing through the gray—away from Noah Adams, Sylvia Poggioli, the droning think tank experts—feels like trudging into the darkness away from a campfire, braced for some scout camp initiation rite.

Brian is an engine, powering away doubts with industry. He sets about getting dinner, rooting in the icebox for the brick of frozen chili. For the first time I get a whiff of the kielbasy, even though I'm out in the cockpit. Many landlubbers may not know how sudden the onset of seasickness can be. Sometimes it attacks with stealth—for hours just a tightness in the sinuses, or the constant urge to yawn. But for certain people an upside down peek into a locker, the discovery of the bilge unexpectedly full, or the garlic radiation of Polish sausage, are instant triggers.

We are about forty miles south of Nantucket, traversing Nantucket Shoals, the vast sandy shallows south of the island. The wind is Beaufort Force 6, sometimes 7 (25–35 knots), nearly a gale. Fortunately it is from our starboard quarter, so we're being shoved, albeit rudely, rather than having to struggle upwind. We're thundering along in the right direction. The sea is what the seamanship books call "confused": our progress is like hurrying through a crowded subway car. The boat corkscrews, lurches forward, stuns back, drops from under us, thuds into troughs, veers.

We're steered by an Aries wind-vane-controlled self-steering device, a spidery contraption hanging off the stern. It is so awkward-looking, its workings are so bewildering yet so assured, that no one seeing it in action for the first time can resist a smile. It is the gear of choice for thousands of voyaging sailors. In these conditions, which would exhaust a human helmsman in a couple of hours, the Aries hauls tirelessly on its steering lines to the tiller, guiding us through the slop like a firm hand on a child's shoulder.

We discuss the broken distance log. The speedometer is working, so we know the little waterwheel that sticks out through the hull is functioning, but the mile counter is not.

"Uhh, just for laughs, a crazy idea, what would happen if we stopped off in Nantucket for a new unit?" says Bob. I explain that it's unlikely the shops

At sea. The blade above the life ring is the windvane for the self-steering gear, which controls lines to the tiller. The gear is so powerful, we must be careful to keep clear of the tiller's swing.

there would have our brand, and each brand calls for a different size of hole through the hull. I control the urge to say, "No, because the rules say we're on our own now." Bob, a New York City fireman on the brink of retirement at forty-nine, has brought aboard a deeply-ingrained sense of rank. Now, and always, he defers to our decisions. He takes the first night watch, nine to midnight, and experiences, to put it mildly, misgivings.

In the morning, I flicker just above the useless mark; we continue to wobble and pummel our way along, making good speed. We put our first daily position fix on the chart of the North Atlantic. Few depictions of life's time are as freighted as that first circled cross. The first note penciled on a symphonic score, first payment on a pension plan, first day scratched off on a cell wall—all hope and risk are in these marks. We *are* only one day out, we could still duck back to Sag Harbor, paint the boat a different color, go underground. But the little voice shouting GIVE UP has been subdued by the planning, the provisioning, the worst-case-scenario safety preparations. Once you read up on various deaths and order things from catalogs to prevent them, GIVE UP starts getting muffled.

For the next two days I battle my despair and regret. Another thing land-lubbers don't know about seasickness is that the most insidious symptom can be black depression. Fortunately, when you are puking hourly, no one expects you to put on a happy face. Not that I don't have other grounds for despair besides seasickness—my cherished hoard of worries for example. But in my queasy dejection, I assume I will remain so until death by dehydration. I peck at cookies. We have brought canned peaches in bulk. During the storm in 1981, they were the only food we could stand.

On that passage, with just us two aboard, we took turns standing three-hour watches through the nights, so for fifteen days, neither of us got more than three straight hours of sleep, and usually much less, since slumber is far from automatic in the bounce and slam of offshore work. We arrived so exhausted it took us a week to recover. This time, with three of us, there's the chance of getting six uninterrupted hours. But I find that, with Bob on watch, I can only manage to doze; he hasn't yet earned my confidence enough to permit me real sleep. In fact, no one ever has but Brian.

The second night, two hundred miles out, we puzzle in intermittent showers through a fleet of fishing boats that are milling around in sloppy seas on George's Bank. Even if our faint running lights are invisible from the bright fishing decks, solitary men with coffee in wheelhouses are watching us sneak across their radar screens. Normally I would find this exotic, companionable. This night I am lying in my berth, grimly clinging to my most recent cookies. Brian calls me on deck. He has disconnected the self-steering gear to hand-steer through the fleet, and needs a hand on the winch. By the time I'm suited up—boots, foul-weather gear pants and jacket, safety harness, lifeline, and lifejacket—I'm lucky to make it to the rail in time. Thereafter any movement—turning my head, never mind cranking a winch—sets off a tremor of nausea.

We leave the fishing boats behind. Rain continues on and off. The wind vacillates in strength and direction so the Aries, which is designed to maintain a course relative to the wind direction, is useless. The seas are random jouncing cones; we are a bathtub boat with giant six-year-olds having a water fight nearby. Even Brian, as hardy and steady as they come, is discouraged by all this, so far from what even the fanatic could call enjoyable. Even Brian, who has not puked in the ten years we've been together, pukes.

The third day and night the wind steadies again; we continue hurtling through the gray monochrome. When not on watch I am an inert, silent, self-pitying lump, hogging one of the two good sea berths. Brian and Bob put up with me; Brian has recovered and Bob seems immune. We've fitted the lee cloths—foot-wide canvas strips along each berth, secured by lines to the overhead—to keep us from rolling out. Chocked-in, splayed, braced, dozing, craving this cocoon despite a low hum of claustrophobia, I endure the boredom of monitoring my guts. I am slowly recovering, but each time the icebox is opened, the gust of kielbasy sets me back. Bob has brought an industrial quantity, in his generous, eager, just now annoying way.

My body puts out a different set of chemicals at sea. My face is as greasy as on an all-night bus trip. My urine is brown, my teeth and tongue are perpetually furry, dirt grows under my fingernails. In my nostrils is trapped a sour, pungent odor, and in the same way you flick a loose tooth or flex a sore muscle, I keep pinching my nose—grimly, obsessively inhaling what I've come to feel is the smell of fear.

On my night watch I take the shortwave radio out in the cockpit and curl up on the low side, in the lee of the dodger, to hunt for the BBC. On that first passage in 1981, from Beaufort, North Carolina, to the Caribbean, listening to a good play was a comfort. The theme music for the *BBC World News* is as strongly linked to night watch at sea for me as Mama Leone's Restaurant is to JFK's assassination. I do locate one of the BBC bands, a weak signal, the voices murmuring through lengths of sewer pipe, accompanied by whoops and basso drones like old sci-fi soundtracks. I fine-tune the frequency knob as though tuning a violin. Trying to snag into the fabric of radio waves, I am not comforted; I brood over the perversity of carrying on straight out to sea.

Sailing across an ocean in a small boat is one of those concepts, like falling in love or making your first million, that seems safe to yearn for. The idea is simply stated; it is not likely to dare us around the next corner. We can gaze at it, adorn it as we wish, without needing to face the details it may include. Over the years, as we carelessly heap it with baggage, it becomes a promise we are making to ourselves, a yardstick for measuring our boldness, a jumble of antidotes for whatever has been wrong. For me, this investiture began almost as soon as I became a self-supporting adult.

As that stage of life opened, around 1968, I was a smart-aleck New York free-lance musician, fresh out of Juilliard, clomping around the recording studios and rehearsal halls of the city in my trademark L. L. Bean rubber-bottomed boots. I imagined that this bizarre affectation was noted with approval, or at least that people said What a kook rather than What a jerk. I was married—I'd known Cilla since junior high school in Ithaca—and as far as she knew our marriage was merely the fulfillment of her pledge, announced to friends in seventh grade, that some day she'd get me. It was sensible; she was smart, funny; we were good friends. But for me, it was an attempt to cobble together an alternative to an insistent and inconvenient truth that I'd been jousting with in utter secrecy since the age of about ten. Our West End Avenue apartment was fragrant from her bread-baking classes. Eighty-pound sacks of flour leaned against the radiator that didn't work in the kitchen, in the living room was her potter's wheel, in the bedroom her zazen sitting mat. We were that offbeat couple.

I played brake drums, lengths of copper pipe, coil springs, and flower pots, as well as the usual battery of percussion instruments, for the Juilliard Contemporary Chamber Ensemble. This job included two summers as artists-in-residence at the University of Hawaii. We had rehearsed all of the repertoire before leaving New York, so the schedule was a few brush-up rehearsals and a concert each Monday night. Cilla and I lived in a tent at Makapuu Point State Park and once a week I changed from cut-off shorts and flip-flops into white tie and tails. She passed those days at the university ceramics studio, where she met a beautiful young man, lean and brown, with long blond curls, who became our buddy for walks along the shore, hopping from rock to rock with his wooden flute bobbing from his shoulder sack. I later learned he'd been more than a buddy to her, and felt not jealousy but envy.

I subbed in the Radio City Music Hall Orchestra. The stage show came after the movie. I'd sit in the musician's lounge with a book—that was my season of Beckett and Genet—surrounded by gray men playing games of euchre that had gone on for thirty years. At the sound of the jet engine roar of the runway scene at the end of *Bullitt*, I would close my book, they would place their euchre hands face down on the table, and we would board the orchestra pit. Then, as we lit into our pastiche of show tunes, embellished with my xylophone curlicues, the pit would thrust us up from the basement to amaze the day's tourists. One day I missed the rising of the pit and had to slink down the aisle and vault the purple velvet railing. Unfortunately, the timpanist was also the personnel manager.

For the Broadway musical *Promises, Promises*, composer Burt Bacharach specified that he wanted the orchestra pit covered over with sound-dampened plywood. Each musician had a microphone; there was a sound engineer in the wings at a twenty-four-track mixing board, and the audience heard the score through huge speakers. Our conductor's torso fit through a hole in the plywood so that he could conduct the singers on stage with one hand, us with the other. Being typical musicians—that is, irreverent opportunists—we dressed in jeans and t-shirts, read newspapers, groaned at the jokes, waged raucous poker wars. When, during the dialogue portions of the play, the decibel level in the pit reached that of a busy restaurant, the conductor would do a deep knee bend, appearing to the audience like a turtle pulling its head in, and plead with us for silence.

At about this time I met a guy who had also gone to Juilliard, had done his Town Hall debut piano recital, and had had a modestly successful, if short, performing and teaching career, all the while yearning to go into advertising. By the time I met Mike he was an ad copy writer for J. Walter Thompson. This appealed to my sense of the ironic; it was the first time I'd heard of a Juilliard product renouncing the calling. And he had a sailboat: a woebegone little sloop that he kept in a seedy boatyard hard by the landfill on Little Neck Bay in the Bronx. There I first got that faraway look in my eyes and discovered how it can take hold even when you are crouched in the mud under a sifting of old bottom paint flakes. We didn't know each other long but there were a few Saturdays when he and his girlfriend and I "took deli" and headed for Execution Rock, pumping steadily. I'd messed about in boats, mostly rowboats, all my life, but this was different, and planted a different seed. When I would talk about it with Cilla, she would show me she got it by saying, "Yes, I feel the same way about mountains."

One day at the hot dog stand in front of the musicians' union on Fifty-second Street, I ran into a guy I had played fraternity parties with when we were both at the Eastman School of Music in Rochester years before. During the time we were out of touch, he had become a successful studio arranger, composer, and conductor. He treated me to the hot dog, gave me a recording date for the next day, two for the next week, and told me to sign with Radio Registry, a studio musicians' booking/answering service. So began a wisp of a career—six or seven hours was a good week—which felt, at fifty dollars an hour, like hitting the lottery.

Any income at all was heady, after years on a student budget. I bought a new 1968 BMW 1600 for $2,477. At twenty-one, I was generally the youngest person on every job. Those around me were talking about buying weekend houses, so to keep up I went to the New York Boat Show. The salesman knew putty when he saw it. I did stop just short of financial ruin in talking with him, but it was somewhere in through there that sailing across an ocean was first taking hold in my dreams.

I was growing disillusioned with contemporary chamber music; the composers defied the audience to enjoy the sounds, which ranged from merely jarring to militantly irritating. My snide cracks in rehearsals nearly got me punched in the face by my fellow percussionist, a true believer who I've heard has since gone mad. When the group scheduled one hundred hours of rehearsal for a diabolically difficult piece by Pierre Boulez, with the perfectionist himself conducting the last twenty, I resigned.

Studio work trickled in steadily: tambourine on two and four in countless Monkees' tunes, vibraphone "sweeteners" on ballad albums, fight scene sound effects for a Mick Jagger film, dozens of radio and TV ads. The music was mostly dumb; the hot dog encounter with my angel had fallen in my lap, so naturally I took it all for granted.

I had had the good luck to dip into many areas of the New York music world in a short time. It is not boasting to say that I did a good job at a wide range of musical tasks. The reason is simple, but it is one of the dark, unspoken secrets: Playing percussion is easier than playing other instruments. There, I've said it. This is something that even the most snobbish and malicious violinist never said to my face, though who knows, it may be something other musicians have assumed through the centuries, passing along a pact never to say it to the faces of percussionists. It seems to me that an adult in formal dress, sitting for twenty minutes counting rests, and then solemnly rising to play a cymbal crash, should at least wink at the audience. Former colleagues will sneer: Sure percussion is easy, the way HE did it. I certainly don't claim that I ever approached the blinding virtuosity on the vibes of a Gary Burton or a Milt Jackson, the tumultuous drumming of a Buddy Rich, but neither do you need to to get the job done in ninety-nine percent of professional settings. For me, music was not a calling, as it was for those monks I saw all around me at Juilliard, who had skipped childhood and now looked forward to lives of rehearsals, concerts, and airports. For me it was an interesting way to make a living, providing occasional tears of joy, many lumps in the throat—more than you can say for most livelihoods. I did not live it and breathe it, and felt increasingly alienated from those who did.

That was a time when, at Be-Ins in Central Park each Sunday, thousands cavorted with rainbows painted on their eyelids, Ginsberg chanted, disciples of Hendrix, Coltrane, Machito, and Ravi Shankar each had their turf, the music a blurring stew in between. I strolled through it like Mr. Mum, with tears in my eyes. I would linger close by a shirtless, sweating conga player, his lean arms tensed, hands a blur, or close by a slim, androgynous guitarist, thrusting out a solo. I was held by the music, but that was not all. What left me mute in such scenes of abandon was the yearning which had pestered, excited, and perplexed me since childhood. After years of internal skirmishing, I had arrived at this tepid truce: My big fun someday would be to stay near this kind of sensual male, to tag along on his life, to have him get used to me and accept my admiration.

Even this prim goal was a poor fit with the life I imagined lay ahead. It set off alarms in me; I was certain it must be kept utterly secret. As for more carnal urges, I worked at keeping them stomped out of mind. At Juilliard the male dancers in leotards and leg warmers I had passed in the halls seemed so at ease with who they were, so settled into ways of being that were definitely not me, that I was able to take comfort from their differentness and go on kidding myself, even as I stole glances at them.

I was determined—got married right in the face of it—not to give in to a path I was sure would make my life miserable. I had never told a single soul about my yearnings. I had never done anything about them; not even any adolescent experiments, perhaps afraid I'd know they were no "phase." OK, there was one single soul I told, but the circumstances were so surreal, it feels like it happened to somebody else.

At that time the draft lottery was vacuuming young men out of their study carrels to feed the Vietnam War. I had applied for conscientious objector status: written the essay, procured the sheaf of supporting letters, spoken before a hearing. It was denied at the local level, but approved by a unanimous decision of the state appeals board. The local secretary was so enraged by this reversal, she scheduled me immediately for an induction physical. She was determined that I would carry stretchers in battle. What to do?

Draft counseling was a minor industry of the era. At any one of countless churches, campuses, and community centers, you could peruse a giant ring binder full of the latest afflictions guaranteed to get you out. Unfortunately, I was in perfect health and was just about the only person I knew who hadn't logged the years in psychotherapy that would merit a convincing letter. Everyone knew the Army didn't take homosexuals, but rumor had it lots of guys were trying that claim and the officials weren't buying it without proof. My careful disguise was coming home to roost.

There did seem to be one glimmer of hope. Word had it that you couldn't be inducted if you didn't complete the physical. It was illegal to refuse to cooperate, but, according to the whispering network, if you said you'd give anything to cooperate, but you just couldn't bring yourself to do such and such, that would be the end of it.

On the day itself I presented myself at Whitehall Street in lower Manhattan and took my place in the grim queue of waxy New York boys in our underwear. I was unshaven and several days unwashed, the better, I'd been advised, to break down my self-esteem, to be in the proper frame of mind for self-abasement. Around me, many men clutched THE LETTER; a man came tumbling out of an ear-testing booth, writhing in pain (that was a guaranteed out); rugged guys slouched about with sloppy mascara. Docile enough through the early portion, I made my stand at the moment I was told to take off my underpants.

The attendant gave me a withering look and sent me to wait outside the psychiatrist's office—my true objective, the chamber where so many thousands of men's fates had been decided. After a long wait, I was called in. The tiny, whitehaired doctor with thick glasses took my papers. While he examined them, I recited my lines about how my acute discomfort at being naked in front of other men had made it impossible for me to complete the physical. The window was open; an air hammer shattered the air outside. I had rehearsed this speech in front of friends who had howled with approval at my stereotyped (and, they thought, preposterous) portrayal of a repressed homosexual. When I was finished, he continued to study the sheaf of forms. Finally he looked up and said "But I see that you have not yet completed the physical examination." With the noise outside, he hadn't heard a word I'd said. He ordered me out of his office.

Standing panicked outside in the hall, my body was dumping chemicals into my system like the can-shaped lump of spinach going down Popeye's gullet. I suddenly said to myself, I am not leaving this building until I flunk. I turned back to his door, walked in without knocking, and unleashed a performance of such operatic intensity, and volume, that, mainly to get rid of me, he finally wrote the magic codes on my forms and sent me to the checkout station.

My true identity having thus saved my skin, I returned to my closet, from there regaling my friends with my story of bizarre imposture. I resumed my habitual absolute secrecy and disguise.

I thought this discretion and chastity counted for something, as though escaping the label was what mattered. But New York kept tossing bait. I could resist the sleaze—live sex shows on Eighth Avenue, rent boys in mid-town—but even posters for the ballet and the mundane coziness of gay couples walking in the West Village drew my eyes and mocked my resolve. If the city was determined to lead me into temptation, maybe I'd have to live somewhere else.

It was around then that I joined half a million others at the Washington Monument to protest the war and Arlo Guthrie greeted us: "Hi freaks!" That night fifty of us unrolled our sleeping bags on the Persian rugs in Senator Eugene McCarthy's baronial living room. The aroma of the cook's chili mingled with the traces of tear gas we wore so proudly. Voices were saying to me, Drop out.

After a while I was let in on the fact that my recording studio angel was having an affair with the wife of one of the producers. This producer was a jittery speedball who sat behind blacked-out windows in his gold Cadillac limousine, abusing substances not yet so in vogue as they are now, before coming up to our recording sessions. He was said to be connected with killers. On the breaks, he and my angel would put their arms around each other, exchange cigars, show off baby pictures. I was given to understand that this was just the first complication I was going to have to keep straight to move on to the next level in the business.

By now, we had traded our BMW for a VW bus. Cilla parked it as though she were the mayor; our glove compartment bulged with unpaid tickets, $40 a pop. She had started Japanese lessons. I was virtually the only person I knew who had not been mugged, having learned a fierce demeanor for the street. It included striding purposefully past men lying on the sidewalk with blood coming out of their mouths. I was becoming mean there.

One day, seeing the cop writing his way up the block, I dashed out to move the van from the hydrant.

"Hey! You!" He ambled up the walk, all mild menace. "I want to see some proof that the summonses that I and the other officers on this here beat have been writing on this here van are being paid, or I'm going to order it confiscated till you pay up."

This was it. But no. Somehow, because of my abject stammering, or because it was too much paperwork for him, he relented: "OK, look. I don't want to see this vehicle, legal or illegal, ever again. Understood?" Maybe it was kindness.

"Yes sir, officer, it'll be in a parking garage in five minutes." It was time to leave New York.

A couple of months later, we emptied the waterbed, sneaked the van around to the front of the building, and loaded everything in, including the potter's wheel and a cast iron double sink I'd scavenged from a demolition site. At the last red light before we got on the West Side Highway, the same cop was directing traffic; we were the front car. My stomach vibrated through the longest light. I shall never know what it meant, but when the light changed, he motioned us on. Nothing, probably. Vermont, here we came. Aside from the marriage bed, my virginity was intact.

2

On the fourth day, bits of blue sky appear; seasickness loosens its grip. I break out of the cabin to stand on deck in the wind and watch *Clarity* charging along. She is so able. We're making such good time. The Loran has stopped flashing. Someone noticed that the distance log is working again. It's hard not to ascribe temperament to these devices. Gradually, it dawns on me: There is nothing wrong here but my fear. I've had this stuck-record question in my brooding: At what point is it crazy to feel this scared of something you are doing and yet keep on with it? Now that question molts to this one: At what point is it crazy to be this scared for this long in the face of perfectly manageable conditions? I fight it. Yeah, but we could hit a half-submerged shipping container any minute and die like puppies in a sack. Yeah, but you could step out of the house and get hit by a bus and it's not considered appropriate to lose sleep over that. Yeah, but out here there's nobody to help you. Yeah, but how is your moping around adding to the general preparedness? Etc.

Brian has had his fill of my gloom. He takes me aside to say he's concerned that I seem unable to enjoy the passage. Of the three of us I'm the only one with this flower-child need to savor and telegraph every misery. Brian is Scottish—moody but not compelled to explicate his moods—and overall determined to make the best of what he has gotten himself into. Bob comes from the Brooklyn streets, where advertising your fears is simply arming your adversaries and resilience of spirit is a survival trait; from a career spent fighting fires, in which self-possession is a matter of life and death; and from countless hours killed in firehouses, where a kind of low-cost all-purpose geniality keeps you off each other's nerves.

By taking me aside Brian brings home to me that my attempt at self-possession has flopped. I've assumed that if I didn't actually stand up and lecture my mates on my regret and despair, it would not be communicated. But by looking out at the ocean like a farmer looking out at the locusts, by glowering at Bob each time he says "So far, so good," by refusing to give in to a cheer-up look from Brian, I've chipped away at morale just as surely.

During this fourth afternoon, the wind gradually drops; the sky clears. We haven't wanted to look at each other or at mirrors—salt-sticky, stubbly greaseballs that we are. We heat water in the kettle and take showers with the pressurized garden sprayer. Finally: fluffy hair, fresh clothes, sheets, pillowcases. It's warm, calm. We start motoring as Brian works on a dinner of pan-fried pork chops with zucchini, chopped onions, and sour cream. Bob suggests—typical crackpot fireman idea—that we shut off the engine and drift during dinner. We humor him.

In this moment the headlong, dogged, agitating dash is broken. Suddenly, quiet: the faint gurgle of leftover waves, the slack shifting of the rig, the water hot cobalt, a still, blue vacuum overhead, a flock of small birds paddling, fluttering, diving nearby. We look at each other. This is the first magic.

We open the voyage's first bottle of wine; Bob serves cheese and crackers. Dinner in the cockpit is superb. Our piece of ocean is ringed by cumulus clouds, as though signaling distant land; we name it Dinner Bay. I try the smile muscles. After dinner a light, fair breeze stirs and we ghost away, doing the dishes, sunset astern, moonrise ahead. I have let go of something. I'm not claiming an instant conversion to buccaneer, but now I am ready to do this.

Murphy has in mind a test.

Bob is on the first night watch. The breeze builds until we are once again well heeled, clipping along at six plus knots. In my berth, I'm sleepily aware that we should change to a smaller jib, for the same speed with less stress. At 2330, a rain squall hits. Bob calls us. As *Clarity* heels to the gusts, Brian and I suit up down below, a lurching tangle of limbs, sleeves, boots, harnesses. I am not queasy. As always at night, we each reach out into the cockpit to connect the safety lines from our harnesses to the eyebolt outside before climbing the companionway stairs. There is a peevish undercurrent. Bob should have called us earlier, when he first felt we could do with less sail. His orders from us were Don't hesitate to wake us. But then I was lying below thinking less sail and not doing anything about it, and his hesitation was only to spare us hassle.

I crawl forward in the pelting rain, clamber over the dinghy to the bowsprit, clip my safety line to the bow pulpit, and brace myself to gather in the huge genny. Brian releases the halyard. The tumbling, billowing sail gets away from me; part of it drags in the water. I haul it aboard and laboriously stuff half of it in the bag before I realize it is wound around the bow rail. Meanwhile the flailing topping lift has gotten around the flag on the end of the man-overboard pole and snapped it off. We stomp the sodden genny into its locker and I crawl forward again with the smaller jib, amazed at how often my safety line manages to lasso my ankle. I hank the smaller jib onto the stay, plunging up and down in the drenching darkness, shouting to Brian when he's to haul. We hoist the new sail and finally fall off onto our course and begin to move again. Brian and Bob head below, leaving me sitting in the downpour. It's now my turn, the graveyard watch—midnight to three.

Within an hour, wind still increasing, I feel we should lower the main and carry on with just the jib. I hate to call Brian out again. I stall. There's also this ship that's overtaking on a similar but converging course, who won't respond to my radio calls. At 0130 another squall hits and I call Brian. There is a peevish undercurrent. Peering into the dark cabin, I can just make out his irritable thrashing. Finally he emerges from the cabin. We tack away from the ship and then lower the main. Brian stumbles back below, his off-watch hours now doubly-nibbled. I sit in the rain. It's warm rain; my foul-weather gear is keeping me dry; adrenaline is keeping me awake. This is an adventure. Who ever said it would be easy to sail across an ocean? I give Brian an extra hour of sleep.

In the morning I dig out the blank book Diana gave me for a personal journal. I begin: "These pages will be smudged and rumpled with the fillips of sea water that penetrate everywhere. It is Sunday, June 26, our fifth day out, the first day that I could even think about doing this."

I sit writing in the cockpit, engrossed in something other than my guts for the first time. The sky and water are clean blues, the shades of a 1950s two-tone Chevy. We're broad-reaching heavily-reefed at top speed through squadrons of thousands of Portuguese Men-of-war, tumbling some in our bow wave. Their inflated sails pop back up in our wake. (Bob, who is partial to things Portuguese, wonders what they are called in Portugal.) *Clarity* makes her busy noises: the scrawk of the Aries steering lines through their blocks, swelling and fading gushing sounds around the rudder, a drying dish towel strumming the lifelines, the occasional rrrap! of spray on the deck. We slow into the backs of the waves, accelerate down the fronts, loping in a soothing long stride.

It is 1492.58 miles to Horta, Faial, Azores, according to the Loran, not flashing. By now we've learned that it flashes whenever cloud cover interferes with the signal. At first we recorded silly quantities of Loran positions in the logbook, flashing noted, sure each one was the last. We had no idea it would still be giving us positions this far out.

Today I take our first round of sextant sights. The purpose—to measure the vertical angle between the sun, you, and the horizon—requires that you steady the sextant, absorbing all the motion of the boat through your body, like a waiter carrying a tray of martinis down a ski-slope. Then, by swinging the sextant from side to side as though it were hanging from a hinge at the top, you make the sun's image in the mirror appear as a pendulum grazing the horizon. Besides swinging, the sun is also rising or falling at an astonishing rate, except at noon. The task is to slide into exactly the same rate with the sextant's fine-tuning knob, catch the sun at the bottom of a swing, perfectly perched on the horizon, shout "Mark!" to the timekeeper, and then read off the angle you have reached. It is a useless exercise before you have your sea legs. And taking the sights is the fun part.

The paperwork consists of averaging the five or so sights and times from the session to minimize error, then "solving" the result by a muttering incantation of dip errors, azimuths, Greenwich hour angles, and other hocus-pocus not necessarily ever understood by the practitioner. This produces a line plotted on the chart and the brave hope that you are somewhere on that line. This line, when manipulated to intersect with those generated by two other sessions during the day, gives you a position called (by some forgotten navigation addict) a running fix. Dredging the paperwork routines from textbook, tables, and memory is pushing it for my stomach, but I bounce back in the fresh air.

Bob's Brazilian wife, who no longer lives with him but remains a good friend, has made us a generous amount of green spice, a Brazilian condiment of garlic, onions, parsley, green peppers, and salt. Today Bob is giving us a foretaste of the Portuguese with a dinner of chicken marinated in lemon, lime, and green spice. I ask whether the spice needs to be refrigerated. "Hilda tells me," says Bob, "Just leave the bottle under the kitchen sink next to the furniture polish."

I'm still not exactly bubbly, but at least doing other things besides brooding. I'm nothing if not stubborn, and Brian's urging me toward cheer has kept alive a churlish flicker of grumpiness. I know he's right though and anyway I probably should at least attempt to stop putting a dent in his adventure. My dreams keep me posted on suppressed terrors. A tape-loop dream of hectic, endless voyage preparations runs like Muzak whenever the main feature isn't playing. This morning I dreamed that the friend who is renting our house was standing in the front doorway, ordering me to sea despite my protests that I was not ready. I awoke distressed, could not figure out

Brian taking a sextant sight. To get an accurate reading, you must absorb all the motion of the boat through your body, like a waiter carrying a tray of martinis down a ski-slope.

where I was. When I did, a wave of panic shot through me, like the instant when you know your car is going to crash and you think This is really happening and Couldn't we try this scene again? But the new outlook said Get up and make everybody a big breakfast, you'll feel better, which was true. And I've regained enough sense of humor to bring off throwing the kielbasy overboard.

The move to Vermont, which brought about a near shutoff of income, set the sailing dream back to zero. But it was in itself as romantic and harebrained a leap as any sailing venture. All my inconsiderable savings would be plowed into building a geodesic dome—a plan hatched when a friend had built one over the patio part of his restaurant on Seventy-fifth Street. To this project I brought childlike notions of carpentry: I had built bookshelves in our apartment.

The site was on land owned by a friend, a situation which would have horrified my father even if Ephraim had not been the Rasputin of northern Vermont. His girlfriend Ginny had been a classmate of mine at Eastman six years before. At that time Eph, twenty-five years our senior, had lured us with jug wine to the Blue Heron, his upstairs art gallery/poetry den near our dorms. Ginny had scandalized the school by dropping out in our first year to move in with him; their seedy apartment had become the hangout for Eastman's tiny rebel cadre. At eighteen my rebelliousness consisted of muttered heckling from the back row of Music Theory class. Sexually anything but a rebel, I had advanced only to dorm room push-ups and sit-ups with two unsuspecting friends. Anyway, Ginny and Eph had stayed together and now offered a hillside meadow.

Before dome construction began we took care of two necessities. Ginny built us an outhouse of scrap lumber, gaily painted by their three kids, and presented it as a groundbreaking gift. I installed a fridge ($5) under a tree on a shipping pallet, plugged into a five-hundred-foot extension cord to their barn. It was stocked with Ballantine Ale, a brew forever linked in my memory to that summer of 1971.

Work began: digging holes for the concrete piers, drilling holes in the ledge, lugging buckets of concrete from the cranky mixer, hefting floor timbers so green they spat at you when you nailed them. It was good to revel in the sexiness of hard work, the stirring that accompanied a heavy lift, good to see the modest definition reshaping my tube-like limbs. My approach to getting things square, level, and plumb involved half-remembered principles of geometry, lengths of string, concessions to the terrain, cheerful shrugs: go with the flow, we're inventing a new world here.

Cilla and I did not truly arrive together in Vermont. Pottery and the Far East called to her and all I had to offer was a mildewed tent and an extinct sex life. After a few days she went off to a crafts school in South Carolina for three weeks. By the time she returned, she'd come to a decision: it was time to move on. I did not protest; nor did I reveal the reason for my re-treating affections—that was still rigidly secret. For a sweet week we shared walks, dinners, night talks, as though courting, pausing every few hours to ask Must it be? and agreeing, in tears, it must. We each had our reasons why our paths had to part, but I kept my most important one from her for years to come. She took the van, I got the dome-to-be. She drove to Seattle and has now been a Zen Buddhist potter in Japan since the mid-seventies.

Word spread, in those days, of undertakings like the dome. Soon, a tiny, feisty woman named Arlene, with a large, edgy German shepherd named Commando, had established a campsite. She wanted to help, no strings attached. In the evenings she sat alone in her tent, crocheting bizarre vests which sold for hundreds of dollars in New York boutiques. The day we were ready to erect the two-by-four skeleton of the dome, ancient vans appeared, people offered their first names and a day's work. At the end of the day, we scampered over the 175 triangles like monkeys, amazed we'd built something strong. I had a ponytail; the sallow, mean ex-studio musician was brown and lean and proud.

That night we had a fire of lumber scraps and celebrated late. I gave myself permission to hug these young men, total strangers that morning, who had spent the day straining, winching, and hammering for me. They thought nothing of it; a hug was as easy as a nod then. But for me, who had main-tained my disguise these many years by monitoring my every touch of a male, this was reckless and fine.

In the next weeks, Arlene and I stapled muslin to the skeleton, filled some of the triangles with Plexiglas for windows, and, one crisp September day, the whole thing was sprayed with polyurethane foam. One pass of the foam nozzle, the hot chemicals would rear up like the head on a beer and go rigid in three seconds. I cut my way in through the front door with a bread knife. It was still warm inside. This would be home for the next twelve years.

That first winter I listened to "Tea for the Tillerman," fed the stove, car-ried water, scratched Frankie the kitten behind the ears. Never, that I can recall, did I regret throwing away a career. Some of my New York friends made their one visit and left shaking their heads: "Where do you go out for coffee?" Some others came with their cross-country skis, their shopping bags from Zabar's, fell in love with Westford, and live in Vermont still. I went to work—just enough to keep the phone and lights working—building houses with a contractor who would look at a crooked stud wall and announce, "You'd never see it from a running horse."

In the last months in New York, with the safety of my impending departure, I had allowed one friendship to crescendo into a chaste romance. Ron was a few years younger, straight, had been a percussion student of mine a couple of years earlier. A teacher-pupil imbalance hung on even after his lessons stopped; it seemed to make us each happy in a way. His contribution—a sweetly sentimental nature—sheltered under mine, a shell of worldly wisdom aplenty for both of us. Gradually, cautiously, I had introduced touch to the picture: manly squeezes of the shoulder, the upper arm; a quick brush across the back. It astounds me now how much I made of these mild gestures, which pass by the million between he-men every day. My obsession with my secret had made impossible that sort of commonplace, so nourishing to the soul.

By the time I left New York we'd reached further; we could listen to Miles Davis or Carole King with arms draped loosely across each other's shoulders. We talked a lot about our friendship, and how important it was. My words were couched in virginal, idealistic language; I don't know which of us was more afraid I might make an unwanted advance. I was raising the stakes, seeing how close I could venture to the dreaded label, exploring the forbidden sensual territory while still maintaining chastity and secrecy.

After I moved to Vermont we mailed each other audio cassettes, murmured with crickets in the background. With the safety of distance, my language became more ardent. New friends in Vermont made gentleness and connection seem a good thing. My New York hardness began a pendulum swing to rural mellowness. Letting myself feel even this chaste passion for a man was thrilling. By the time Ron came to visit after several months, I had lost the will to keep us both feeling safe. The manly squeeze lingered a second too long; the brush of fingertips took on an exploratory quality. We each caught a whiff of danger and backed away, forever awkward after that. I'd aimed the friendship where it couldn't go and lost it, stumbling as I first let the compartments of my life open to each other.

I began to want to tell someone my secret. The time was right. I was on my own and had no more need to shield my marriage. My new friends were avowed flouters of convention, and talk around kitchen tables was often of the search for wholeness and happiness. With this crowd it was hard to stay convinced that my confession would taint me forever. Who would be the first to hear? There were a couple of straight men I had private crushes on, but after Ron, that seemed too thorny. Ginny felt safe.

Over weeks I worked up to it, actually thinking up lines. In the end, I still couldn't plain be out with it. I purred about my new life in the country, how in New York I used to avoid eye contact with strangers and now I hugged them, how I was discovering touch. Then I added, seemingly as an afterthought, "I guess I'm just one of the lucky ones who can be turned on by anybody." I was simply claiming a racy new skill, layered onto my presumed straight virility. She was sweetly unruffled, gently left silences for me to fill; before long we were reminiscing about handsome freshmen at Eastman.

In the spring, Judy Zappia moved to town. She had just graduated from Fordham, loaded her tent and sleeping bag on a bus, and said good-bye to Brooklyn. Her total plan was to join her friends Scott and Kathy, who were living in a tree house in Westford. Scott was the third man on our carpentry crew. Dropping him off one day, I met Jude. Sitting around the picnic table, we one-upped each other with obscure New York jokes. I had to move to Vermont to meet my equal at imitating middle-aged housewives from Brooklyn. She was saucy and profane, and carried her boyish body in a light, springy way. I felt stirrings of desire. Perhaps here was a woman I could be happy with? The next day, they all came over to the dome for dinner. Jude was apparently impressed by my gesture of scooping the congealed leftover spaghetti from the bowl and flinging it down the meadow, because she stayed for six years.

I told Jude right from the start about my attraction to men. (By then I was admitting it was physical, and not just a desire to hover admiringly near them.) I used the same sort of breezy, omnisexual line I'd used with Ginny, though admitting I'd had no actual gay experience. Thus misled as to the grip of my sexual drift, Jude was unfazed; it was just another exotic detail of her new hippie existence. We agreed I might need to explore this some-time. How lightly we set out together down what was plainly (to me anyway) a dead-end road, and the longer the road, the more painful that end. What impelled us was genuine and powerful, but for me it was love with a hole in it. In our reckoning, we let the naughty, eccentric allure of the match outweigh its potential for sadness.

Those years have a shapeless quality in my memory, unpunctuated by achievements. We were truly broke all the time, and fretted about how to get the checking account up to zero. I'm not saying we ever knew the despair of poor people. Being broke was a choice—not to say, with grumpy hindsight, a pose. We were trying to break the cycle of make more money so you can pay people to do more things for you so you can have time to enjoy yourself. We basked in the empty time, ate what was ripe, made our Christmas presents. Our equation was off sometimes. We squandered time with the endless firewood-gathering and the crouching in frozen driveways, pop-riveting a flapping fender. But I learned which way a tree will fall, how to drown the cabbage worms off the broccoli for dinner, how to loosen the distributor and turn it till the engine sounds right. I felt more at home in the world, more hooked to the sources of my life.

Summers we weeded and went to Jeffersonville Gorge, where rednecks could sometimes be seen standing in the bushes with a six-pack, looking at the hippie girls. With Jude as my camouflage, I looked at the boys. We spent one summer, feet up out on the deck, watching the Watergate hearings. Winters, Jude smoked and knitted and read; I played music and, in between spasms of my lower back, tried to keep ahead of the stove. Bit by bit, my livelihood reverted to music: teaching part-time at the University of Vermont and Johnson State College, and playing timpani in the Vermont State Symphony Orchestra. I built a bedroom addition that was square and level, and a garage that was used, from the start, only for Ping-Pong.

One day I was washing dishes when a friend from up the road walked into the dome. Glancing into the mirror over the sink, I saw she had with her a man so staggeringly good-looking that I thought surely when I turned around and looked right at him, I'd realize the mirror had been playing tricks. But no!

Barb had picked up Pierre, just in from France, hitch-hiking by the green in the village. He had come to locate an American he'd met in France years before. Going by his scrap of paper that said "General Delivery, Westford, Vermont," he had arrived at Kennedy, taken a bus to Burlington, and hitched. He had already found out from Kevin at the store that the man he sought had moved away long ago, so he was at loose ends, looking for a place to stay. I grinned. How about dinner for everyone and we'll figure something out?

Jude was equally bowled over; we often shared the same taste. At dinner Pierre talked about his girlfriend Martine. Oh well. After dinner, Barb was tired and headed home; Jude finally faded off to bed. Pierre and I sat swapping life stories. After a while, he said, "I don't know what it means, but I have zeese dreams where I am wiz a man and we are in bed . . ."

That night my fingertips first explored the silky skin of a washboard tummy, a trespass the center of me had been longing for since third grade, regardless of whatever more socially-approved longings my brain had supplied as cover. In the morning I waited for the crushing tidal wave of guilt and remorse. Nothing. We all went to Jeffersonville Gorge, where Pierre floated motionless in the shallow pools, catching trout with his bare hands. After a couple of days, he headed off to continue his tour of America. The world seemed to me full of promise.

There were quite a few of us homemade householders in Westford; by and large, we all got on well with the local folks. In all of Chittenden County, which includes Burlington and is Vermont's most populous county, Westford was the only totally rural town. The old-timers liked that just fine; they worried more about invasion by the IBM-ers from the 6,700-employee facility in Essex Junction than they did about a few longhairs. A few of the old-timers had a bit of a renegade glint of their own. Dan Jackson, who'd lost a leg as a boy in the sawmill up the road, had nonetheless ridden his Harley to Alaska. Roland Pigeon, who wasn't allowed on the schoolbus as a child because he's French-Canadian, now owned all the schoolbuses. He was proud, in a kindly way, careful not to judge people who are different.

Of course we were never more than out-of-staters. If you were born in, say, New Hampshire and moved to Vermont at a week old to stay for a hundred years, the obituary would say "so-and-so, of New Hampshire, died today." In Westford this wasn't ugly xenophobia, just a bland fact. At that time, there was a ritual, since declared unconstitutional, requiring new residents to appear before a Council of Elders for approval before they could get on the checklist to vote. At the time Jude appeared, the council consisted of three men: Jimmy Grow, about seventy-two, whose two grandfathers had owned the feed store and the general store on the common; Rob Mannings, about sixty-five, who, when you stopped at his "Sweet Corn" sign, would walk you into the field to pick it fresh; and Harold Dahl, a squinting curmudgeon whose wife taught harp in the UVM music department. Jude and I were known to be cohabitating, but Jimmy's genteel vision arched gracefully over such private matters and Rob counted us as fellow lovers of truly sweet corn. With a scowl of distaste, Harold leaned toward her: "Says here you're from Brooklyn?" "That's right," said Jude, cheekily. Harold leaned back and glanced at the other two with a what-more-damnation-do-you-need look. "How come you came to Westford, then?" he asked. Rob cut in, "Well, gee, now, Harold, didn't you come up from there about forty years ago?" Color crept up Harold's neck; the interview was over.

Eventually, although I was still driving rust-laced junkers and approaching the official poverty line from below, my credit rating offered a choice: a septic system or a sailboat. That first boat was a thirty-year-old Luders 16, a narrow sliver sixteen feet long at the waterline, twenty-six feet overall, with two canvas pipe berths in her tiny sitting-headroom cabin. I named her *Chanterelle*, after the mushroom which was abundant in Westford. From the date I acquired her my vegetable garden grew smaller each year.

I began to cruise the coves and islands of Lake Champlain, finally putting flesh on the fantasies of sailing away. Very soon I knew that what had drawn me to Vermont—the urge to be self-reliant, to simplify my life, reconnect it to its sources—was what sailing offered as well. Of the people who adopt sailing away as an image of escape, many end up finding the reality to be an anchoring squabble per day with their mates, or vein-popping racing competition as draining as Monday through Friday, or the edgy boredom of slowdown shock. My uninformed fantasies, by luck or intuition, felt more on target the more I explored them.

3

Another perfect day, and another; reaching, reading. Brian and Bob confer on fishing tactics. The population of the Atlantic Ocean has utterly shunned the researched and expensive tackle collection Bob has contributed. He remains optimistic: he is now up to two rods and is detailing specific sauces he prefers.

Every couple of days or so a ship's derricks, then superstructure, then hull, break the horizon. Or at night, a white light, at first looking like a low star. Then, recognition, and the tense wait to make out the red or green lights, to reckon its course. Headed for us? Ranked with storm, fire, injury, and major illness, is the fear of being run down by a ship. A ship can reach you from the horizon in fifteen minutes. Some sailors leave it to their radar reflectors, trusting that passing ships' crews glance up occasionally from their Kung Fu videos to their radar screens. Single-handed sailors, for example, must trust that to get any sleep. Even with a radar reflector, we keep watches all night. The man on watch may be reading down below, the Itty Bitty Book Light clipped to the pages, but he must stick his head out every quarter hour for a scan of the horizon. I sometimes doze clutching a kitchen timer. We call each ship on the radio; most answer. English is the international language of radio, but we find the night shift's English a bit rusty on most ships. We ask for a position check and a high seas weather forecast, which is carried on a frequency that our radios cannot receive. Some officers are chatty. On the way to the Caribbean in 1981, I looked up from my book one afternoon to see that a ship, which I'd noted earlier was passing safely distant, was now headed right for us. I jumped for the radio to find that the ship's captain had headed over just to be sociable. As we talked he made a large circle around us, then headed back on course for Senegal.

The wind builds each afternoon; we take another reef in the mainsail. We leave the reef tied in for the night, just to be lazy, and shake it out each morning. Course and speed barely vary, day after day. We're covering about 125 miles each twenty-four hours.

It's our eighth day. I write in the log book: "Only complaints: bulb loose on Itty Bitty Book Light, too much sun on Brian's berth at naptime." The nib on the recording barometer continues to trace a straight line across the top of the paper. We are in the Azores High, a giant fair-weather system which sits all summer every summer in the North Atlantic, centered roughly on the Azores. The days are hot, clear, breezy; the nights warm and gentle, as though we've entered a *Popular Science* Perfect Weather Zone of the Future. We have the main cabin hatch open all day and night for the first time ever at sea. We've slung a towel tied at all four corners under it to catch the occasional dollop of sea water. This gives the cabin a Bedouin air. We lounge in the cockpit and below, reading, sunning, snoozing. We shower every other day. Lunches are sardines or smoked oysters, maybe a soup, one or two cheeses, crackers, olives, pickles, mustard, horseradish, cold beer or seltzer. Dinners are elaborate affairs; the meat courses and casseroles are still coming out of the icebox with frozen centers and at least half of our ice still remains. The Gulf Stream is with us, adding perhaps a knot to our speed over the bottom. That bottom is so far below us I try not to think about it. The endless procession of cumulus cotton from horizon to horizon makes it hard to believe that the whole world has not fallen under this benign spell.

With the lifting of my gloom comes a return to our normal friskiness, and Brian and I catch our pleasures, working around the watch schedule and Bob's naps, the modest muffling of the groans adding an extra spice. It's not that Bob seems uncomfortable coexisting with us; he's gone out of his way to reassure us, albeit by feigning shock and dismay, followed by hearty laughs, each time talk takes a gay turn. It's more a gesture recognizing the inescapable cell we share, and the need to keep off each other's toes. "No, but seriously," he concludes, with a favorite line, "You know me— one foot in the closet and the other on a banana peel."

On this eighth afternoon, we speak to the container ship *Gulfspeed*, bound for Savannah. I say we're bound for Scotland, and her Swedish-sounding skipper tells us he has family in Dundee. "It rains a lot there. That's why they invented Scotch." But that was the former climate of the world, right? What do we care. Later on I catch myself sniffing around for my quota of worries and fastening on the waters around Britain. But fifty million people live there, I tell myself, and every shopkeeper and schoolteacher has some kind of blunt little boat; it can't be that dire.

We celebrate: halfway to Horta, a thousand miles to go. Gift bottles of champagne are stashed everywhere below; we must start celebrating more often.

Brian is high on this. Normally reserved, he exclaims now at each new pleasure, immersed in the shipboard routines. Whether he is solving his sextant sights, making a stew, or fine-tuning the fishing tackle, he's as lost in it as a boy building a model airplane. There is no impatience to get the task done, but rather an ease about following it where it leads, a gift that is a passage-maker's dream.

Brian and I differ most in our relationships with time. We agree it is more precious than wealth, but each of us wrestles to control it in a different way. Time tricks Brian; it speeds up whenever he's not looking, meaning whenever he has his laser focus on what he's doing, which is nearly always. In his work as a pediatrician at Yale–New Haven Hospital, time sneaks to a gallop; there is never a chance to make a dent in the work. Come Saturday morning, he announces we will paint the house before lunch, he just needs to work on a research article first. At three o'clock he surfaces, outraged to find his day stolen. I, on the other hand, make sure, with tact and subtlety, that we get places on time. I drop the guillotine on conversation if it's time to leave for the movie. I lobby for undertaking less. I shun pressure. I hoard book-length stretches of leisure, but slam the book closed when it's time for the news. Even sailing as we are in perfect, benign conditions, I can't quite lose myself in the present. The part of me that knows what time it is won't completely stop worrying. Looking back on a safe voyage will be my moment.

It has always been this way with us. I've always admired Brian's energy and devotion to the moment. I've always been exasperated by his refusal to accept how long things take. He's always admired my determination to carve out free time. He's always been exasperated by my throwing the timekeeper's wet blanket on his plans.

Over time, Jude and I felt our paths diverging. Our ambivalence showed in the legislation we adopted—you can have an affair but you have to be home in bed by morning—that tried to free us yet keep us held. For me the policy was mainly theoretical anyway. We would stand around the margins of parties grading the men, all straight, and agreeing on them. We were each yearning to allow a sexual adventure—"side action" was our bravely raffish term—to deepen into a connection with future.

Once I was ready to be with, rather than just look at, a man, I had to face the fact that there were roughly seventeen gay men in the state, or so

I reckoned peeping out from my closet. I had tried turning up the warmth with a few of the straight men I had crushes on. A couple were flattered, a couple edgy, none interested, none—to their credit—violent. One, a rangy blond folksinger, personified grace under pressure. I was publishing songs at the time, and wrote a wistful ballad, with gender-neutral pronouns, about my unrequited feelings for him. Despite knowing he'd inspired it, he volunteered to learn it and sing it on a demo tape for the publisher.

Roaming the Burlington bars, which were booby-trapped with friends who didn't know about me yet, I had tried to work up to eye contact with total strangers, no doubt all straight. I'd glance carefully for hours, marvelling and quailing at the power of my eyes to draw his—a futile pastime, possibly dangerous. Perhaps I just needed some of this dummy trolling drill to acquaint myself with the basics of the hunt, before I tried it in a setting where it might actually have consequences.

The Taj Mahal Indian restaurant opened its basement bar to gay men one night a week. The owners, who loathed us and never mixed, collected the cover at a card table by the door, making change from a steel box by the light of a fluorescent desk lamp. Within: red light bulbs and disco. Presiding was a flamboyant queen named Donny, always in a western shirt, jeans, cowboy boots; a wig of blond curls, operatic makeup, long fuchsia nails, bracelets, a cigarette. He dished noisily all night from his throne at the bar, but was a generous, gentle hostess to wary newcomers like me; he chose a few people for me to meet. I'm not shy, not cowed meeting the important, but if desire is the reason I'm introducing myself, I feel it's written so plainly all over me that it would be preposterous to talk about anything else. Since I'm too prim for that topic, I'm most comfortable remaining mute. But at the Taj Mahal I was determined. So this was the first experience in my life of talking about the weather with other gay men where we all knew what we were. The banality of it was reassuring; it helped me withstand the hungry looks from unwelcome quarters. I waited in vain for one of these chats to feel like a discovery. I could grow old waiting for him to step into my life in Vermont. I needed density. In Montreal, an hour and a half to the north, they had gay bars by the dozen, said the Burlington boys. Just walk in and pick, I imagined.

It took me several years to prepare myself for the overwhelming wickedness of that possibility. This was so utterly shallow. Just go for the best-looking man in the place? What is this about, sex? In the meantime, I waited boldly to see what men would show up if I just led my life. One chilly fall day I picked up a hitchhiker with a sign that said MAINE standing on a road leading out of Burlington. It was getting dark. I asked him if he realized how far it was and advised against setting out. (Hmmm, nice smile.) He listened to my advice and said, "In that case, can you tell me if there's a gay bar in this town?"

A cloud of butterflies left their perches in my chest. In the silly, deadpan way I have when I'm nervous, I suggested we go have a beer.

Peter lived in New York, in the East Village, and worked in a restaurant where the waiters entertained by juggling lemons. He was on his way to visit his parents in the small Maine town where he'd grown up. His eyebrows danced, telling me. A boyish, unknowing sexiness lit his moves. He bet me he could teach me to juggle. A few minutes later I heard myself invite him home for the night. "I'll drop you on my way to work tomorrow," I said, "fifty miles closer to Maine." I was in uncharted territory now. Jude and I had never done anything like this to each other.

By the time Jude got home, Peter had taught me to juggle. Jude was careful, textbook friendly, as though she'd known this sort of thing might be in the cards, and now bore it steadily in case she should want me to do the same for her sometime. Peter taught her to juggle too. Quite early she said she was tired and left us alone. The cats were confused, and checked on us every couple of hours. I crawled into bed with Jude by morning. Side action had come home.

Out of this, Jude and I had a talk—"Must it be? It must be"—like the one I'd had with Cilla years before. Through many tears we agreed to throttle back to best friends. I was blinking out from under my camouflage to let the world come at me. This time was I finally ready?

Jude moved into the room over the garage/Ping-Pong parlor. This last had still never had a car in it and had recently been converted to a silk-screen t-shirt printing shop for her latest venture: Comfort Graphics. She joined me in the dome—which at least had a stove and sink—every morning for breakfast, and most evenings for dinner.

That winter I drove to New York four or five times. Peter was the first man I ever traveled to spend entire weekends with. Before long, we both knew it wasn't going any further and agreed to let it taper off, but the simple pleasures of returning to a man, waking up with him, were building in me.

On my first trip to Montreal, I walked directly from the train to a newsstand for a gay paper to find out where the bars were, and there was the headline: 138 ARRESTED IN SWEEP OF CITY GAY BARS—19 FROM VERMONT, 31 FROM NEW YORK. I caught the next train back.

I calmed down for around a year and then tried again. This time I drove my Chevelle to midtown, parked, and began the rounds. Three big dance bars were within a block of each other. I slouched from one to the other, receding steadily into myself. The one person I worked myself up to talk to turned out to be a militant Quebecois, who would not say so much as Hi in English. When my eyes burned too much from the smoke, I would break for fresh air and move on, returning to each place several times.

By two A.M. I was wrapping up my dud adventure in the one called The Studio. It was up a flight from the street, with a dance floor to the right— dark, large, jammed, earsplitting—and a bar to the left. The bar was an oval in the center of the room; men did their slow, watchful laps. I was at my post, the sort of lookout cats prefer, just outside the flow, vantage point for the cruising oval, incoming traffic, and the fringe of the dance floor. I hadn't spoken to anyone in hours. My eyes were red orbs; I looked like I'd been kept awake in an experiment.

The tongue-tied hours had given me time to think. What made me think anything would happen the first time? I'd probably have to make dozens of these trips. And the real question: Just because Jude and I had conceded that our futures weren't together, was I really now looking for that kind of a partnership with a man?

Just then a tall, slim, black-haired prince appeared at the entrance wearing a tweed jacket and loosened tie. Now HE was why I was here. For forty minutes he moved, paused, spoke with friends. No backslapper, but his smiles to each were big and kind—the face of a shy, polite man working hard to be cheery and outgoing. I'm drawn to upbeat men, but don't much look like one. It would be nice to be able to look jaunty and intriguing at times like this. Instead, my eyebrows arch, my forehead furrows, as though I were staring down at a faulty servant. Once or twice: eye contact at thirty feet—both of us wary, grave. Getting on toward last call. This was it.

I shifted to a position at the bar where he would have to pass close by on his next lap. Closer and closer he came. I took a deep breath. This mattered. Must speak. Ready . . .

"Hi."

"Hello." A British accent. He passed on by with a pained smile. I wheeled to the bar in confusion. Without thinking, I rubbed my smoke-fried eyes nervously, opening the tear sluice as though I had stuck a sliced onion under each lid. Oh, great. I dabbed at them with my sleeve. He had gone across to the edge of the dance floor. I approached the pounding disco din. To get him to hear, I would have to scream at him—never attractive—so I tugged at his coattail. He turned around.

I motioned for him to lean close. "It sure is loud!" I hollered.

"Yes, what do you say we move along?" he said, and strode off toward the door.

We swept down the stairs to the street. He hailed a cab and we were off before I could decide whether to tell him my car—the Chevelle was not impressive—was parked around the corner.

We went to his midtown high rise. Even in the glare of the elevator he was handsome—eyebrows of character, a strong-willed shock of black hair, a contained intensity of manner, aristocratic but determinedly friendly. His apartment was small, tidy, grad-student functional, but with a few oil paintings. Despite the selection process that had brought us here, some conversation would be necessary. As we interviewed each other, he was gentlemanly, slightly formal; he spoke through a smile of genuine shyness. My abdomen hummed like a transformer; I struggled to keep the flutters out of my voice. The routine facts being exchanged had a bizarre irrelevance to the voltage in the room, but we soldiered on. He had stopped at the bar for a beer after working in the emergency room at Montreal Children's Hospital. In his living room, I spotted a volume of prints by the yachting artist Beken of Cowes. He loved sailing and told me about a cruise with friends among the Western Isles of Scotland. He had elegant, strong hands, always in motion. One flew out and landed on my shoulder. We moved in slow motion. Looking back, it's tempting to claim we recognized the need to imprint each moment.

A couple of mornings later, I was just waking up back home after getting in late when Jude came up the ramp to start the coffee. With a groan meant to sound ironic but actually full of hope and apprehension, I said, "Jude, I think I'm in love."

At that time, Brian was finishing his residency at Montreal Children's Hospital. He'd been in Canada four years, following medical training at the University of Glasgow. He had already roamed North America a good deal and was more and more inclined to stay, if a way could be found. There is an old saying that there are more Scots outside Scotland than in it, and his family was no exception. He was born in Trinidad, where his father worked for the British Colonial Service as a microbiologist. At nine he moved to

Honduras, and at eleven he went off to the Keil School on the banks of the River Clyde near Glasgow. (Just off the Caribbean island of Mustique, in the Grenadines, stands the wreck of the liner *Antilles,* showing so much she looks almost afloat, but broken in half and bottom ripped out from a drunken turn onto the coral reef. She once carried the boy Brian to Britain.)

Suave though he had seemed at the bar, Brian was even newer at letting his gay self out than I was. Any interest in the other boys at boarding school he had ascribed to understandable hormone squalls in girl-less captivity. In university days, he needed only to look at flamboyant queens on the street to know he wasn't one of those. Since less conspicuous gay men weren't identifiable, he never sensed any gay life in his surroundings. I should have been infinitely more sophisticated, having gone to Juilliard with frankly gay and exotically beautiful dancers passing in the halls every day, but, once I moved to Vermont, I had been just as blind as Brian to the gay life around me.

For years Brian's gay side was unreinforced, submerged under medical studies and duties, but persistent and gathering force. If he found himself drawn to a man, he'd say to himself, I just want him to be my friend. But the word "homosexual" would leap out of a magazine page at him. He told me about a family gathering where he was trying to act nonchalant watching Nureyev and Fonteyn on TV, but when an uncle harumphed and shut it off, he couldn't bring himself to protest.

Eventually we each sought a city, trusting it to offer settings where our invisible kind could distill themselves from the population.

By the time we met, I was a known subversive held in wary regard by the more conservative faculty members at my two music departments, pop-music harmony being to them an oxymoron and the Jazz Ensemble I conducted holding scant claims to legitimacy. I engaged in such heresy as encouraging my students to laugh with me at our rickety system of notation, jury-rigged over the centuries to keep up with changes in music. Professors Pappoutsakis, Weinrich, and Swinchoski saw nothing funny about an E double-sharp or a double-dotted sixty-fourth note. Such things had been good to these men. On the weekends I played timpani for the Vermont Symphony. A heavy week was twenty hours.

I had so far remained closeted in these settings, but being with Brian made me want to shout to the rooftops the reason why I had become more lighthearted and confident, and why I had taken to ironing my shirts. Shouting it seemed unwise, but with those students who became friends, I began to find ways to refer to Brian in sly wordings—"my partner lives up in Montreal and he . . ."—which, if the listener were paying attention, would be the tip-off. The Jazz Ensemble was the coolest thing at Johnson State College, so as its conductor, I was a minor celebrity of the remote, hilltop campus. After telling the first few students I didn't need to mention it anymore; word came back that the truth about me was a privileged bit of lore about the place, passed on only to those who could be trusted. It seemed a good outcome: at least those students would head into life understanding that there would always be gay people carrying on incognito all around them.

On Brian's first visits from Quebec it was a fringe tuft of Americana he encountered, meeting our colony of highly-educated carpenters, goat farmers, saloon musicians, and organic pickle-canners. Our homemade houses showed that a person with a college education could retain enough common sense to create a rude shelter. We shared a serene disregard for our expensive training. Indeed, the more esoteric the training had been, or elevated the post we had held, the more heroic was our turning away from it.

Brian had been educated in the British system, where the dreaded O-Level exams at the age of sixteen pruned your youthful scholarly enthusiasms to the strongest two or three shoots. Then, at eighteen, the A-Levels simply said yes or no to your entering university. Compared to the States, only a small proportion of British students are granted this opportunity—none of this "finding yourself" for the first three years of college. And none of this back-to-the-land stuff either. Higher education was too great a privilege. The British counterculture of the time was almost entirely an urban phenomenon, squatters in vacant buildings in London and such. The sharp demarcations in that society are one reason. Just as the vast majority of people are shut out of the professions by their A-Levels, the skilled trades are closely controlled by an ancient apprentice system. A British conservatory graduate does not idly decide to build houses in Scotland. Detours from life's prescribed paths are taken much less lightly in Britain. Here was a Brit on the coveted medical track faced with Vermont's quintessential detour gang.

At our volleyball games little kids, pregnant women, and a few mellow nudists lectured any athlete types who showed excessive zeal. Each household had a spare car for parts moldering in the tall grass, a pile of egg shells, grapefruit rinds, and coffee grounds near the back door, referred to hopefully as compost.

The dome had suffered from sheltering a young man who, under heavy peer pressure, had dabbled in being a pack rat. Free, broken typewriters;

free, broken stereo components; aesthetically pleasing engine parts; water pumps needing just the one gasket; valuable scrap lumber; tires with one more summer on them (were I ever to get a car with that wheel size again). A kitchen/living/dining area had been shouldered free inside, like a movie set interior created in a hangar full of war surplus goods. My well went dry every August; bathing then was in the Brown's River. In rainy times, the furniture arrangement in the dome was dictated by the leaks. The garden harbored rampant Jerusalem artichokes, sunning cats, weapons-grade zucchini.

At Thanksgiving, twenty-five of us sat down on unsplit stove-length hunks of tree trunk at a banquet board made by bridging a sheet of plywood from the Ping-Pong table to the round oak table. Jude and I would do a turkey and guests were to bring the absolute best dish they knew how to make. To some recently converted Manhattan professionals, this meant refined, delicate hors d'oeuvres—a tray of chilled poached eggs in molds of jellied consommé with suspended sprigs of watercress comes to mind. To the more militant pinkos, it meant a kasha-groat-bulgur mash that would survive the day untasted. To one sheet rock taper it meant lime jello cubes tossed with tiny marshmallows. Some toasted with tequila and some started off with the brownies, because they took an hour to hit you.

Winters we trudged up each other's long drives, left our boots in a pile, and danced in thick wool socks to the "64 Greatest Motown Hits." A winter party ended with impaired people loudly pushing each others' cars out. Every Thursday evening at the dome six of us—all refugees from New York— relived its casual bloodlust with a game of Oh Shit, Hearts, or Liar's Poker. Every Sunday evening a jam session with four or five area jazz players filled the dome with amps, drums, electric keyboards, and me and my vibes. The tradition from the start was that we would simply begin from silence with free improvisation, no jazz tune underlying it, listening carefully, hunting. While much of the music achieved only frenzy or density, at least once each night we found something together and ended with tearful hugs. At winter's end we boiled maple sap on our kitchen stoves till the ceilings dripped; we rooted around in our freezers and tried to stay off the roads till Mud Season gave way to Spring.

My urge to show Brian off overrode caution about my privacy; friends would open their doors, take one look at the two of us, read "couple," and that would be me, out. Not one friend betrayed the slightest trouble handling it. To be with friends, finally out, and happily together with a man meant that, for the first time, I was openly whole—even more than whole now, Brian my complement. Routine stuff for anybody who's been in love, but for me, a first experience of whole-heartedness.

Brian wore a bemused smile much of the time those first visits—learning to dodge debates on herbal remedies, marching uncomplaining to the outhouse with a broom for the snowy seat. He gloried in this gust of new friends, despite the fact that our rowdy, untidy lives ran smack into his precepts. What made us think you could just call yourself a cabinetmaker and set to work? Or just have fun and let the future take care of itself? Didn't we care what other people might think? And what about this hugging people when you greet them? And shouldn't we check the curtains before we kiss?

Brian's comparatively courtly manners sometimes cowed us bumpkin posers, not that he intended to. He clearly relished these visits, even if he did have a bit the air of someone carrying on quite well in the bush. And his manners were not at all an affectation, simply genuine, considerate, and British. In an American, though, such manners would whisper of aristocratic pretensions, something we in our greasy down vests were defining as opposite to our own. Yet here he was in our midst, dancing like a Trinidad boy at our parties, and letting our false assumptions about him give him an edge at Liar's Poker.

On one of his first visits in the fall of 1978, he and I were heading out the driveway to go for a walk when we came upon Jude's new boyfriend, on his hands and knees, digging a hole next to the garage, with Jude looking on from her deck. Carrying out a ritual remedy handed down from Jude's Czech mother in Brooklyn, Tommy was burying a potato that Jude had rubbed on a wart. In the instant that Tommy looked up into Brian's polite smile, everything lighthearted about this half-serious endeavor suddenly seemed impossible to explain. Tommy never recovered; Jude and I have always marked that moment as the beginning of the end of that affair.

Brian was a bridge. I had to admit that his civilized manner called to me; I felt drawn away from my studied funkiness. With his visits I first dimly realized that I would not choose to live out my days in rustic squalor. Hiding within me, temporarily subjugated in my goatpen surroundings, was a reasonably tidy person, appreciator enough of fine things to have set in motion the building of a yacht.

Clarity was at this time a hull with a few interior bulkheads in place, in a boat shed behind builder and designer David Stainton's house in nearby Williston. *Chanterelle* had gotten me hooked but she couldn't take me where the dream was leading.

Fortune had smiled on this new enterprise, right from my preposterous application for a boat loan. For a construction loan you need collateral, since the project has no value at first. The dome would have to be appraised. Its foam exterior had been abraded by avalanches, roasted to powder by ultra-violet radiation, and pecked by chickadees going after the ants that infested it. The thinnest parts seeped continually. I had glued strips of inner tube to the edges of the windows in a vain attempt to staunch the rivulets that poured in at each rain. At the base of each window, a garbage bag diverted most of the flow into an old sap bucket. Below one window I'd resorted to drilling a drain hole through the floor. The leakage had rotted crucial por-tions of the floor and its underpinnings. The sink and tub water drained straight onto the ground under the house, maintaining a perpetual swamp which reared up in frost heaves in the minus forty degree winters, jacking the concrete support posts, snapping floor joists, and rumpling the floor to the topography of sand dunes.

The day of the appraisal I vacuumed the gaps between the floor boards, swung the broom through the worst of the cobwebs overhead, cleaned the dried cat food off the end of the kitchen counter with a cabinet scraper, more and more certain that my dream of having a boat built was about at its end. Seeing the first Oldsmobile ever to pull into my driveway, I selected a Mozart piano concerto from the few records not destroyed by snow blow-ing in the cat door, and went out to meet the appraiser.

He had stopped about a hundred feet from the dome and was admiring the view. "I just love the country," he said. Was that a New York accent I heard? A window of opportunity. By the time I'd told him about how I'd gone to Juilliard when it was up by Columbia and we'd ascertained that my old apartment was near his sister-in-law's parents', we were both leaning on the front fender.

"So they say you want to build a sailboat," he said finally. His tone sug-gested we were now a couple of bank defrauders through with the small talk.

"Yeah, I sure hope to," I said.

"I'd love to do that," he said, a Mickey Rooneyish little-guy-with-a-dream look coming into his eyes. "Get me some bimbo, head off, palm trees, down in the islands." His hips swayed.

"Well, it's been a dream of mine for a long time," I said shamelessly, "and I finally said to myself 'Stop dreaming and go for it.'"

In a trance, he raised his clipboard and began filling out his form. He never went a foot closer to the dome.

That flim-flam accomplished, I blundered ahead. David Stainton had never built a boat before, and no design of his had ever been built by anyone. He was an architect who, by agreeing to this project, was turning away from his career, and as it turned out, was risking marriage and solvency. We are still friends, something not all boat-building clients and builders can claim. He now owns a boatyard in Maine, where he has hull number two of *Clarity*'s design under way, but there have been bumps in the road.

The boat in those plans looked just right to me, but I can't say I spotted the design for surefire; I was too much a novice for that. I took the drawings to Bill Luders, a household name among sailors and the designer of my first boat. He made one suggestion on the keel profile, David accepted it, and we were off. Building was to take a year. It took two. In this corner was the champ timekeeper of the hippie era, torn between eagerness to get her wet on schedule and the growing realization that she was to be something very special. In the other corner, an unbudgeable perfectionist.

David has genius traits; I suspect his I.Q. is off the scale, but it's his knitting together of the universe that I mean. His demeanor is certainly not erudite, though he can hold forth on Schubert one minute and crab traps the next. As at home as he is in the world—masterminding his small town's successful fight to stop an eighty-store shopping mall, yarning with dock geezers—he has a distracted air most of the time. It's as though he were a chameleonic martian, sent here to vacuum the landscape for tidbits of knowledge and to try out a few earthling roles. When not in his normal diffident yet gregarious mode, he can be grumpy, fiercely silent, or cantankerous. Money seems a deeply alien concept, as though in his briefings before landing here, he was told everything about it except what it actually is. He goes through life assigning a small portion of his brain to all pestering earthbound concerns while the rest grapples with the unknowable.

As David began *Clarity,* there was a preternatural assurance about even the first steps. In his huge hands (he stands six six) the plane would lift a curl of cherry the length of the board. When it was time to cast the keel, he knew to melt the lead in an old bathtub over a wood fire and convey it to the sand mold using a length of angle iron as a sluice. He knew that the slurps of lead spilled on the ground could be axed to hunks and thrown back in the tub, that the loose stones welded in would float to the surface. He knew the curve to laminate into each deck beam, each slightly different, each minutely adjusted with shims on the gluing jig, each dropping into its mortises with a tap. He knew how to carve a six-foot steam-bent oak tiller, square at the rudder end, becoming an eight-sided shaft, tapering to a round shaft, tapering to a ball. And he knew to surprise me with it.

Meanwhile, at the dome, the gear heap grew: anchors, chain, cushions, non-skid dishes, kerosene lamps, folding bicycles—I called my UPS man by his first name. The cruising fund was getting seriously depleted.

Up to this point, my crew member in the planned sailing venture was to be Paul Sokal, who'd brought his one-burner camping stove and instant oatmeal on *Chanterelle* many times. Paul was then a saloon musician just beginning the transition to real life. He was having trouble saving for his share of the expenses, and given my own cash flow, it was becoming a delicate subject.

About then, six months after I'd met Brian, he left Montreal to begin a two-year fellowship at Yale. He officially immigrated into Highgate, Vermont, with a rented van full of furniture, helping the officials figure out their new ID camera. His parents lived in the States. He was given a green card because of his status as their unmarried son.

By then, *Clarity* had been a year in the building, and I was adjusting to the idea that there would be no launching that season. Though I could well use the extra time to build up savings, it was still disappointing. Paul was getting cold feet about the whole adventure; I was starting to consider the crew slot open. Brian's fellowship would end in June 1981. Everything was pointing to one answer. Perfect. Still, I was out on a limb asking the question.

"How about a year of sailing before your first staff appointment?"

"Sounds quite good to me," he said.

In that instant he agreed to a detour from his British medical track. But more, we agreed to take a step we had each been inching toward since childhood. *Clarity* would be our first home together.

During the second year of *Clarity*'s construction, I spent more and more time at David's shop, sealing, sanding, undercoating, sanding, painting, sanding, painting, sanding, painting, every inch of her interior; varnishing the cherry, ash, and oak trim; bolting down winches, hatches, cleats—any job that just took persistence. David and I were chummy most of the time, merely civil at others. By this time, we were into overtime but it was not in David's nature to raise the price. To keep his household going, he began taking more and more marine surveying work, examining boats for buyers, sellers, and insurance companies. So, a vicious circle: the longer *Clarity* took, the more surveying was necessary, the less progress, the longer she took. Each time Brian was due for a visit, I'd police the boat of scraps and clutter, vacuum the sanding dust end to end, make time to install something special: a brass oil lamp, the hand-carved number board. I'd rattle off the paltry progress, wincing at his disappointment. David's wife Barbara began a term of shuttle diplomacy, relaying word of my growing impatience, returning with word of his growing tension. As much as anyone, Barb enabled *Clarity* to be completed with David and me still friends.

Finally, August 8, 1980, was to be launch day. Brian, David, and I took turns on a single come-along, winching *Clarity* out of her building shed. Her cradle wobbled along a path of planks on rollers made from lengths of plumbing pipe. We kept the planks climbing, more blocks of wood under each one, trying to raise her up to the level of the flatbed trailer. David chain-sawed up all the scrap timber around the place; we built Lincoln-log trestles. After a whole day of it and about twenty gallons of lemonade, she still wasn't high enough. We resorted to digging holes in the lawn to lower the wheels of the trailer. It was suppertime before we cinched her into place on the trailer for her trip to water.

It wasn't until the next morning, August 9, 1980, that *Clarity* was christened by Barb's and David's daughter Lilo at the Shelburne Shipyard. Lilo's first whack with the champagne bottle merely knocked the bottle out of her hand. It was my first emergency as skipper. My reaction was not promising: paralysis. How dare this ritual not go smoothly? How can we mitigate this omen? Brian, without a second's hesitation, dove into the harbor, as he has so many times since, when *Clarity*'s karma has hung in the balance. He surfaced holding the bottle, to applause from the dock. Lilo dashed it to bits on the second try.

Looking back on what a gem David was creating, it seems so clear that I should have just acknowledged it and calmed down. Patience was never my strong suit. Whatever amends can be made by noisy gratitude I have since made. The public holds a stereotype of sailboat owners as sentimental, lavishing a downright goofy amount of affection on their boats. For this I am known, even among sailboat owners. And I've extolled her in numerous articles about our travels. (If Barb thought that at launchtime she might reclaim David from his shop, she was wrong. He emerged from the creative triumph and financial debacle of *Clarity*'s building to design and build an oversized racing bicycle on which he became New England Veteran Champion.)

A couple of days later, we anchored in Burlington Harbor for a Launch Celebration. *Clarity* squatted low in the water under the press of Vermont friends. Brian and I took turns rowing dinghy-loads out from shore, to our party.

Journal entry, June 30, our ninth day out: "Tonight for the rare time I suspended the what-if what-if chorus of worries and let the moment in. Sitting in the companionway listening to Tchaikovsky's Sixth on the Walkman while a full moonrise dead ahead did its shift from melon to cheese, the tears came: tears of release of all the pressures of getting ready, tears of the same sympathy with the music that I felt for it twenty-five years ago when I discovered it, tears for the overwhelming sensuality of the moment.

"In my ambivalence about undertaking this passage, I said to myself, well, I'll just do this last big cruise to Europe, get this out of my system, then I can say I did it, didn't betray my dreams, and I can get back to the cushy life home in Guilford with strictly low-key jaunts to Maine on tap. Tonight the pull of shoreside life is getting set back to zero."

4

Journal entry, July 1, our tenth day out: "While the world buries its head in the sand, Portuguese Men-of-War are massing in the Horse Latitudes for a takeover."

This day is a turning point for me.

I have the last night watch, 0300 to 0600, my least favorite as we've rotated duties, and not only because it's beastly to haul yourself out of a warm berth at that hour. In my life ashore, that is the hour when, if I have had too many liquids, dreams of fingers in the dike give way to a half-awake stumble to the bathroom. Returning to bed, I have a fifty-fifty chance of getting back to sleep. Equally likely is that I will think I've found a lump in my groin or think my heartbeat sounds different thupping in my ear against the pillowcase. Or I'll realize my life hasn't added up to much—friends from school are playing at the White House. Whatever the reason, butterflies stir; the brain works up to red alert; I toss till dawn. On the boat, the dawn watch deposits me at this hour in the cockpit, groggy and vulnerable, to stare at a minimalist scene at once soporific and filled with menace. I'm prey to thoughts of waterlogged dock timbers, adrift since some forgotten monsoon in Java, bristling with rusty spikes, lying in our path. Or thoughts of some rigging fitting (if only I knew which one) that has vibrated loose to the last thread and now lies useless, waiting for the first strain. One defense is to try to doze down below, braced sideways on the chart table seat on a couple of salt-clotted cushions sacrificed for the purpose. At home I fall asleep with difficulty and awaken at the slightest noise. Happily, on this passage, that trait has relented, perhaps because I am functioning at a level closer to exhaustion than I realize, what with the constant demands the boat's motion places on muscles, guts, and psyche. I snuggle the kitchen timer to my cheek so I won't miss the quarter-hourly lookout for ships.

This dozing may still the worries, but it also sets two of my other mental ponies pulling against each other. First, morning is my favorite time of the day. Second, if I'm awakened by an alarm, I wake up grumpy. So with each ding of the kitchen timer, I hoist myself out of the lounging station and up the stairs, and scowl at the first rosy suggestions of dawn. As each fifteen minute doze passes, I wake up grumpier; the dawn is lovelier. Part of me is saying, Hey, come on, look how sweet it is, but as any grouch knows, that only makes it worse. So I usually end up giving Brian or Bob an irritable jostle at 0615, asking to be relieved. I climb into the still-warm berth and close my eyes to the first rays of sun, feeling both put upon and wistful. Such are the perverse ways ennui perpetuates itself.

But this morning is different. At 0600 I make coffee and take a mug up on the deck with the *Audubon Field Guide*. The early sun is warm; there is a light, steady breeze. I sit reading about the stinging strands that dangle below the Portuguese Man-of-War's inflated bladder, strands sometimes fifty feet long. I look up the small black and white birds which are almost always in sight. During the day they keep their distance. At night, they flirt with the big bird *Clarity*, wheeling close by with a bat-like flutter, now and then clucking softly. I find that they are called Wilson's Storm Petrels, and that they are possibly the most numerous species of bird on earth. I read about Shearwaters. In those first days I stared gloomily at their soaring, envying them for belonging here. They are large birds, with brown backs and white undersides that on sunny days flash turquoise reflections of the water. They rocket up from behind a wave as though launched from a submarine, their wings locked in a stretched M, bodies rigid except for their flicking heads, and then they bank into a fast glide, one wingtip grazing the water.

I raise Brian and Bob with the aroma of bacon, and lay on grapefruit, pancakes, maple syrup, and coffee. During breakfast we are slowly overtaken by a container ship. We leave the radio on and they call us. They are bound from Los Angeles to France. By the second cup of coffee, the breeze goes light; we need more sail. Bob proposes that we take a swim between lowering one jib and raising the larger one. Brian is eager, in fact nearly always eager, to get naked and wet. My readings about venomous tentacles are too fresh; at any one time there are ten or twenty Portuguese Men-of-War in sight. Besides, many sailors who are, unlike me, avid swimmers near shore, nonetheless have a fear of sharks offshore that keeps them from swimming on passages. So, with much jaunty talk about how they always come up and sniff you and butt you a couple of times before they bite you in half, Brian and Bob dive over the side. Holding the camera in the air, Brian treads water backward and snaps *Clarity* in mid-ocean. In the picture I look like a father watching his child's first time in the deep end of the pool.

By the end of the swims, the breeze has all but died. We start motoring.

With just the small leftover waves, the horizon seems sharper, more distant; our blue disk of sea is so huge the thought of manually steering across it is ludicrous. With the usual apprehension I dig out the electric autopilot from where it's chocked in the forward cabin. The autopilot is a motor-driven extendible arm that attaches with a pin on one end to the side of the cockpit, the other end directly to the tiller. It is meant to steer a compass course by means, to put it briefly, of an idealistic hookup with a photoelectric sensor. Our experience with this one has been typical for the brand, judging from the fact that the company gave up making them after a couple of years. On the way to the Caribbean, we had just this, no windvane self-steering gear, and it truly seemed put aboard by dark forces, like a computer virus. Whenever a wave knocked the boat more than a certain number of degrees off course, the autopilot became hopelessly befuddled and steered every which way hunting for the correct course, sending the boat into uncontrolled jibes or backward sailing antics. In addition, the unit's excessive current drain necessitated running the engine for hours each day to charge the batteries. By now we have come to use it only for motoring long distances in calms. This we do so rarely that the machine has time to work up a good corroded sulk between uses, and never fires up without a fight.

Thinking to placate it, I attack the usual problem before even trying the switch: I clean the power supply electrical contacts with an emery board and WD-40. Then, try it: nothing. So begins the most fearless disassembly of the device I've ever undertaken, in which I discover engineering pranks of the sort that kept Jaguars in the shop all those years. Brian steers, bantering soothingly, hoping to avert my usual stifled tantrums at such repair-proof objects. But, for some reason, as I back the screw out of the panel that says "There are no owner-serviceable parts behind this panel," and hear the tinkle of various linkages and springs dropping down inside, I remain not only calm, but amused. Brian may well be growing concerned. Is this the first warning of incipient mental breakdown?

Never having seen the innards before, I can see nothing amiss now. I root around with the probes of the voltmeter, a testing device that I use about as effectively as a dousing rod. After much blind fiddling, I do get the motor to whir, though only in one direction. With great effort, I manage to reassemble the whole thing, and unperturbed, I put it away still not working. This is nearly unprecedented. Usually by now I would have mentally composed a seething letter to the company. But we are here, it is not working, we will get by, my anger would be useless. How sensible; how rare.

Scrabble at sea. What better place to figure out what to do with four u's?

A light breeze comes up and we resume sailing. Since the Azores archipelago lies right in the middle of the Azores High, we expect a large area of no wind as we approach Faial and so need to conserve fuel.

Lunch is chunks of leftover steak in a lentil stew with hot pepper sauce. After lunch the breeze dies again; we motor, playing Scrabble. The breeze comes up; we sail, loafing along at three knots.

Suddenly the water erupts in porpoises, a pod of twenty-five or thirty all around us. Some cruise a ways off, others rocket in from abeam like torpedoes, others tumble under our bow. There are young, tagging in perfect synch alongside adults. We scramble around the deck, snapping, pointing, exclaiming. I perch at the end of the bowsprit holding the camera upside down. The animals roll onto their sides just ahead of the bow wave and fix me with a mild, smiling glance. I can hear chuffs of air as they break the surface. One, with a muscular shimmy, jumps clear of the water and does a belly-whopper, soaking me. Those humans on sailboats are sitting ducks for that one. The pod stays about an hour; I spend the entire time on the bowsprit. There is no mistaking that they are playing. I feel as though I've stumbled into a party where I know no one and everyone is singing; I can't stop smiling but there is the slight wistfulness of the outsider. Finally they can be polite no longer; we're just moving too slowly. Abruptly they are gone, leaving us on a nearly calm sea that is emptier than before.

Dinner is a chicken stew with rice and pickled Brazilian hot peppers, another from the arsenal of incendiary homemade condiments Hilda has sent with Bob. An Italian ship, bound for Boston, crosses the sunset, and then I'm off to bed. What was my turning point? The smell of fear is gone.

In the spring of 1981, I worked through lists and lists of lists, preparing for our yearlong cruise to the Caribbean: lists of engine spares, rigging spares, spices, flags of Caribbean nations, charts, celestial navigation tables, candles, solvents, Zip-Locs, tools, novels. I screwed emergency sail track on the mast for the storm trysail. Brian chased down the contents of the medical kit— going to sea with a physician is a great comfort. He didn't challenge my gear choices and expenditures, even though some, like the patented grabbers for climbing the rigging, betrayed an excess of shopping momentum. Though we'd considered ourselves together for almost three years by then, and this would be our first home together, *Clarity* was still, in a way, mine, and Brian was the guest, or at least not yet quite the equal partner. Perhaps there was

51

in the back of my mind the thought that, in the event of a meltdown between us, she was my fallback position, *my* home. At any rate, he was gracious enough to realize I'd been the sole tender of this dream for so long I'd probably not welcome anyone, even him, barging in, presuming instant co-dreamer status. We stowed a roll of ripstop nylon and colored magic markers for making the flags of any unexpected republics. In went the folding bicycles. Finally *Clarity* was ready for her first big cruise.

I had rented the dome to former students from the Jazz Ensemble and arranged a year's leave from the orchestra and both teaching jobs. Brian's fellowship was ending soon. *Clarity* headed for the salt, down the thirteen locks and sixty-two miles of the Champlain Barge Canal with a couple of friends helping me out as crew. We used her tabernacle to lower our own mast, without need of a shoreside crane, for the first of many times. Then into the tidal Hudson River estuary in Troy, past Albany and West Point. Brian and a load of friends came aboard in Tarrytown for the triumphal first time through New York Harbor. It still seemed to me almost a comical leap, shedding the funkiness of the dome for the pristine elegance of a new yacht. Various superstitions—pride goeth before a fall, that sort of thing—whispered in my backbrain as I watched these friends, who in hindsight I can see were on similar cusps in their lives, sampling life after mildew. In my memory, Brian's new day-to-day presence at my side is on the same page as that leap.

We spent the remaining weeks of June living in a Connecticut marina while Brian finished work. During that time, Brian's parents, who had long since become U.S. citizens, were about to relocate from near Boston to Connecticut, and his mother happened to pass through on a house-hunting junket. By coincidence my parents were also visiting, staying in a nearby motel. A waypoint in any couple's path: the parents first meet. I remember very little about the evening we all spent together, but an odd flavor lingers in recall. Our parents are all perfectly sociable people, adept at the graces of first encounters, and the two of us had spent jovial times with each set of parents. Yet, among the three gathered that night, there was a slight, uncharacteristic chill—nothing conscious, I'm sure—a wary holding back, a reluctance to wade into everything this gathering signified, as though warmth among them would equal comfort with us. They don't happen to have ever met again.

Also living in the marina was a young couple who had built their thirty-two-foot ferro-cement sloop. With the wry detachment one assumes when referring to an old wound, they told us the story of their going to sea. When their boat was finally launched after several years under construction, they decided that for a shakedown cruise they would sail to Bermuda. Eighteen hours into the passage they were both sprawled seasick and useless on the cabin sole, unable to navigate, hoping to die without any more fuss. After thirty-six hours, they looked at each other and asked, Have we ever been more miserable in our lives? Is there anything that could be worth feeling like this? They turned around, slunk back to Block Island, anchored, and succumbed to deep gloom. It was the first tale I had heard of anyone coming so close and yet abandoning sailing dreams. I shivered. To this day the two of them, now with a son, live aboard year-round in New England, but rarely sail.

Set free on the Fourth of July, we made our leisurely way toward Maine for the summer, learning about fog, currents, shipping, and the utterly engrossing life aboard a traveling boat. Brian and I became a smooth team, swapping roles on every maneuver until taking a reef or changing a jib required hardly a word. We learned, when going ashore, to tie the dinghy so that it neither ended up hanging from its painter on a falling tide nor hauled under by its painter on a rising one. Observing the ways of other sailors, we both learned and hooted. After watching how often arriving crews poisoned the anchorage and their own cocktail hours with anchoring squabbles, we adopted a policy we still observe. We don't speak while anchoring—hand signals only.

Friends had shaken their heads in disbelief at our intention of making a sailboat our first stab at living together. "It'll be a pressure cooker," they said, picturing a little Alcatraz, patrolled by sharks. In fact, our household was the harbors, breezes, night and day skies, small adventures and explorations of each day, endlessly new surroundings in which to learn each other. From the start, we instinctively understood the special requirements of coexisting in the confines of the boat. If I were writing in my journal, Brian would putter about as though I were absent. If he were reading on the forward berth, I'd do the same. Just by our mutual consideration the boat acquired additional private hideaways. And when maneuvering in the narrow spaces of the cabin, there were no "pardon me's" and "excuse me's," which only serve to keep the limited space on the mind. Just turn sideways and pass.

By the time we set out, we had been commuting to visit each other every second or third weekend for nearly three years. Again, well-meaning friends had sympathized about that hardship. But in fact, the distance had kept the romance, and the voltage, humming. We were always together for leisure time, with news to share, rather than the routine "How was your day?" "About the same."

But mainly we needed those three years to get used to each other, and for each of us to get used to having a man for a partner. We were both proud, stubborn, and accustomed to calling our own shots; there were many tug-of-wars in the early days. Sometimes it took the whole two weeks between visits for ruffled feathers to smooth, for absence to make the heart grow fonder. (I griped to Jude; she said, "Please! Where are you going to find somebody else that cute?") We were learning to accept rather than rail against each other's immutable quirks, to accommodate, to puzzle through the sort of pecking order questions that straight couples lump under the heading Battle of the Sexes. One quirk of mine that I would have sworn was immutable vanished utterly: I am no longer ticklish. When I was a boy all that was required to reduce me to a cowering, cackling, pleading mess was my older brother's index finger waggling within two feet of my rib cage. Now the stark danger of light touching had been transformed to bliss.

We sailed our first overnight passage, from Nantucket to Boothbay Harbor, spending most of the first night virtually motionless in the middle of the Gulf of Maine, earnestly unaware, happy enough to be pointing at the right star. The second night we fell in behind the distant stern light of another boat that seemed to be heading, as we were, for Seguin Island light. Gradually it dawned on us that what we were seeing *was* Seguin light, and that the capital "F" on the chart meant "fixed light," rather than "flashing." We proceeded up into Boothbay Harbor in the wee hours, motoring blindly through the thousands of lobster pot floats, protected from a snarled propellor by the patron saint of beginners.

For six weeks we cruised the shattered peninsulas and islands as far as Northeast Harbor, eating mussels, raspberries, blueberries, and for the first time knowing the thrill of sailing to places truly wild and remote. When it was time to leave Maine I knew I had just tasted what would be a lifelong feast.

In the fall we headed back through New York Harbor and down the New Jersey shore to the Chesapeake. As we sailed along the straight Jersey beach, I did my first sextant sights, placing us somewhere in West Virginia. In Mannisquam, New Jersey, I chatted up Tom Tyne, the guy on the next boat, who complained that, since his wife was writing a seafood cookbook, he was going to have to try three sauces and two different stuffings with his flounder that night. Brian and I helped out. Tom and Barbara, their Persian cat Jo, and their springer spaniel Sherman were headed for the Bahamas to run their boat in charter. For the next few weeks, until we parted ways in North Carolina, we often met up and traded dinners, Brian and I much the gainers. It was our first itinerant cruising friendship, a sort I've come to prize.

We shared the creeks of the Chesapeake's eastern shore with oyster tongers and acres of Canada geese. We learned a dozen ways to get a keel unstuck from the mud—swinging the boom out and doing pull-ups on the end of it from the dinghy, tying a masthead halyard to a distant anchor and winching her over—all the while taking it not too seriously, like kids building a dam, like my first Vermont forays into carpentry.

On the western shore, we anchored in the middle of downtown Baltimore; we wedged ourselves up Spa Creek in Annapolis and went ashore to beat on a pile of crabs with little hammers.

Toward the end of October, frost on the deck in the mornings drove us southward, merging us with the annual migration down the Intracoastal Waterway, through the Dismal Swamp Canal, the Pungo and Alligator Rivers. But while most of the others were looking forward to a boulevard run to Florida, we were starting to look at The Big Time: our first offshore passage, fourteen hundred miles from Beaufort, North Carolina, to St. Thomas.

There were plenty of others anchored in Beaufort Harbor who were, in the peculiar phrase, "going down outside," and a fine camaraderie welcomed us. The maritime museum had an ancient pickup truck they lent free to sailors for provisioning runs; they showed us what to do if the gearshift stuck. Everywhere urgent talk about the weather: we were all going to be rolling the dice between the end of the hurricane season and the beginning of the winter storm season. Around the parts counter the sailors and the locals talked of how and when to cross the Gulf Stream.

One night the guy from a tired old sloop nearby rowed over to talk. When they'd left Newport he'd told his girlfriend they would motor down the Waterway to Florida, but now he was bored and had decided to go outside. She was absolutely against it, but that didn't matter he said, he would just singlehand the boat while she stayed below. "I don't mind getting wet as long as it isn't cold." Brian and I exchanged a glance. His friends had teased him because, the first time he sailed the boat after buying her, she sprung a garboard and had to be towed in by the Coast Guard. We urged on him the need for joint commitment. How far can you go cautioning a total stranger? We alluded to the nickname of the waters near Beaufort: "the graveyard of the Atlantic." I felt as though we were talking him in from a high window ledge, yet sailing is one arena of life where committing dangerous folly is a hallowed right rather than a sign of lunacy.

One morning, the forecast abruptly turned rosy; we awoke to the sounds of boats maneuvering around the town dock to top off their water tanks. It was time to go. After a hectic few hours of laundry and final provisioning—not easy on a Sunday in Baptist Beaufort—we motored through the anchorage toward the channel. Our new friends waved us on with crossed fingers and promises of rum punch rendezvous in the islands.

Four days out we were clobbered by the storm. There's no need to recount here how I climbed the ratlines with a sabre in my teeth and screamed at the wind, daring it to blow harder. Suffice it to say it was the first time in my life I ever spent several days thinking I might die any minute. In the middle of it I seriously asserted that when it was over we would head for the nearest point on the coast and put the boat up for sale.

The real lessons came in the looking back. One of them was that my love of sailing could actually bounce back from such a low. *Clarity* had shown us she could take care of us; survival was retrieved somewhat from the realm of superstition. Some people sail offshore for years without ever getting hit, all the while worrying that the odds are building up. Not us. We had gotten that out of the way right off. A storm was now something we could picture.

There was another more important lesson, something soldiers know: the bond left by facing mortal danger with someone. In the middle of the three interminable days of howling wind and toppling gray mountains, without speaking about it, Brian and I each focused on one thing: the fear of losing the other. In the exultant first day afterward, when we had wet gear drying on the lifelines like celebratory flags, Brian told me that he had known he did not want to survive if I did not. I had known the same. We would get each other through it. Life changes when you have felt you would give it up for someone. No matter what follows, you and that person hold that moment in common forever.

With just the two of us to cover watches, with the capriciousness of the autopilot, and strong headwinds for the last six hundred miles, the passage was exhausting. We arrived in St. Thomas after fifteen days and collapsed. Others from Beaufort were already there or straggled in after us, veterans calling it the worst storm they'd ever seen. We'd gotten off light. Others had suffered major damage, some had limped into Bermuda; a ship had gone down. The guy and his reluctant girlfriend had been taken off their sinking boat by a naval vessel, before the storm.

For nine days we sat at anchor among the giant fleet in the rolly waters of Charlotte Amalie, looked down on by the cocktail lounges of the day's cruise ships. Finally we were fortified enough truly to begin our cruise of the Caribbean.

We headed for the north side of St. John. Turquoise passed beneath *Clarity*'s keel; the looking-over-our-shoulders feel of being at sea softened into cozy anticipation.

In our first anchorage, I saw my first dead body. We were out walking on the beach when a jeep came bouncing toward us. The driver shouted, "Are you a doctor?" Brian said yes and the driver directed us to a knot of people farther along the beach. Then he zoomed off to get the National Park Rangers. Running up to the group, we found a man on the sand, already going gray. He had been found on the bottom after he'd gone snorkeling alone and drunk. Brian quickly, quietly set to work: first he set me into the rhythm of pounding the man's chest; then he cleared the mouth and began mouth-to-mouth resuscitation. For an hour we worked, to no avail. The man's family and friends held each other and wailed in anguish. There was never a pulse, never an unaided breath. Finally the rangers arrived and loaded him in their Land Rover.

Back aboard we were quiet, I regaining my equilibrium, Brian more accustomed to seeing death but still sobered; both of us waiting for this shadow to move off. I was struck that sometimes being alive seems so sturdy a state—people hang on through months in hospital, dozens of operations—and other times a life just winks out.

July 3, our twelfth day out. The wind has died completely. Overhead: cumulus-flecked blue nothing. Hour after hour, the leftover ripples have rounded off their creases, flattened, like the brushstrokes in setting varnish. Underlying this quieting surface, though, are the softened remains of giant waves from a storm near Iceland, now low dunes, hundreds of feet from trough to trough, heading for Antarctica.

For all its tranquillity, I find the scene a bit spooky. It's hard to see how any weather could ever get to you. Don't die, diesel. But we expected this. These are the Horse Latitudes, so named because sailing ships, becalmed for days and weeks, would throw the horses overboard to conserve water.

Even I swim. Let the record show, however, that, an hour later, we see two dorsal fins, *not* porpoises. We motor all afternoon. At one point we alter course to inspect what looks like a floating log but turns out to be the merest fraction of a basking whale, with a sidekick nearby. They sound and shortly appear on the other side of us. My heart works OK.

At dinnertime we shut off the engine. Drifting to a halt, *Clarity* begins to roll in the swell, with great commotion from the rig and the pot locker. We don't linger over our seafood bisque. All around us, as usual, the slowly heaving surface is littered with Portuguese Men-of-War. In the late sun they look like pink and blue glass flea market butter dishes. Soon we motor on our way.

Last dusk, a mirror sea. A wall of clouds to the north looks like it might be the cold front promised by a couple of ships' forecasts—maybe some wind. I line a star up with the rigging to steer by, and lounge with the tiller pressing lightly on my ankle. Behind us is the next to last minute of deep copper; ahead the horizon has disappeared, the stars and their reflections are indistinguishable. We are a space module with a noisy two-cylinder diesel, out for an evening spin from the space station. Every few minutes I click the flashlight on to check the compass, then immediately off. Most boats have a red compass light that doesn't destroy night vision as white does. Ours was a casualty of disuse. I know that Brian, dozing below, may well be hearing the flashlight click on, waiting for it to click off: a signal that all is well. When I am off watch at night, the first click penetrates my sleep, and I awaken in the absence of the second.

Clarity has never spent a night at sea without both Brian and me aboard. Over the years other crew members have stood their night watches and doubtless assumed they were allowing us rest. But I sleep deeply only when Brian is on watch; my utter trust in his judgment lets me go. When it's my turn to sit out here, I think of the duty less as an act of self-preservation than as a gift protecting my sleeping man.

Gradually the oncoming clouds ink out the stars. One by one I lose my bearing stars, until the darkness becomes that of a sensory deprivation chamber, no up, no down, the vastness invisible. A peculiar thrill tickles the back of my neck, takes me back to the moment when you have just pulled the cover over your hide-and-seek place and you don't know if you can stand the dark waiting.

With nothing to head for, I must see the compass. I contrive to sit reading with the Itty Bitty Book Light shining on the compass, my knee holding course against the tiller. With my night vision thus wrecked, when I look up every fifteen minutes to scan for ships, the shell of black surrounding me seems so close, so opaque, I could be sitting in a thermos bottle. Only if I look aft can I tell where air ends, water begins, by the phosphorescent globules in our wake.

On one scan, my eyes finally adjust to reveal a faint light ahead, not a point but a patch. A lone ray of moonlight on the water? An undersea volcano? Will my story be in checkout line tabloids? I get out the binoculars. It is a bar of light, well up in the sky, cast by an invisible moon against cloud. I have lost all sense of the horizon.

I resume reading. The book is *The Wild Boy of Burundi,* an anthropologist's account of a famous case of a boy believed to have been raised in the wild by monkeys. Scientists battle with each other and with African health officials for access to him to test him, poke him, train him. He is neglected on wards, set out in a sort of kennel. There are rumors of hoax; he may be just another abused, abandoned child. Because he is sullen and uncommunicative with his examiners, some pronounce him not truly feral, but merely mentally ill, perhaps autistic. I study the photographs of him: the numb, closed face, the self gone from the surface to some unreachable safety within. At this moment we are as isolated as it is possible to be on this earth, a sense heightened for me by the feeble parasol of light and the absurdly loud clatter of the diesel. I have chosen this and find an eerie peace in it. This boy has not and does not.

In the middle of the night, I sense that the faint breeze on my face from the boat's forward motion has become a real breeze now gently but steadily from abeam. I slow down to be sure—yes. I call Brian and we raise the big genny; the main is already up. I shut off the diesel. *Clarity* heels slightly. The booming silence is gradually filled by the hiss of bubbles in our wake. I adjust the Aries to the new wind direction and shut off all lights. Black peace.

We knew the Caribbean would be palm trees and turquoise water; those had been lure enough during the Vermont winters (if not during the storm) and we weren't disappointed. We spent a rich tropical winter learning the particular feel of taking our home from country to country. What we didn't expect to find was what turned out to be the best part: friends.

In all the months we had spent cruising the east coast, Tom and Barb Tyne were the only people we had really gotten to know. Most of the other sailors around us were on their week or weekend, absorbed in family or friends on board, headed back to the home port soon. We did meet a few people who were on longer cruises, but because we were going in different directions or at different paces, the day-to-day continuity never took hold. We were surprised to have met only one gay couple; we'd assumed the autonomous sailing life would be a natural draw. Even those two guys weren't actually cruising. Each year they worked the summer as waiter and bartender in Provincetown, then motored down the Intracoastal Waterway to work the winter in Key West.

In the Caribbean there were, besides the locals who hauled cargo from island to island, four clearly defined groups of sailors, with little intermingling. First, the bareboaters, down for a vacation on a rented boat: pallid, carefully hatted, to be feared in close maneuvering. Second, the crewed yacht professionals. These were a hard-working lot, maintaining their boats to a high standard and providing the best of food and aplomb to their clients. In between charters or owners' visits they regaled each other with stories of the time the King of Spain stepped off the gangplank into the harbor and so on. Then there were those cruisers who, like us, were doing a one-winter circuit of the Lesser Antilles. And finally, there were the lifers. Some, stern-to in St. Barth's with weed from their hulls reaching the bottom, still thought of themselves as traveling, though the engine, disassembled under a tarp on deck, would have to be sorted out. Others, moored alongside a homemade parts barge in St. Thomas with a jumpy mutt patrolling the decks, may truly have given up—may have sold the mast to buy cigarettes.

We quickly learned to recognize our kind. There was often a certain zestful overkill to the boat's equipment—steps up both masts on a ketch; three small outboards clamped to the stern rail; lovingly elaborated sun awnings with rain-catching gutters, wind scoops, detachable side curtains; a row of jerry jugs lashed on deck, originally red but now faded to the color of those wax chewies full of syrup. In each boat you could read the savored anticipation that had gone into the preparation. Despite the prodigious array of oars, boathooks, anchors, ladders, lines, sails, sailboards, buckets, and bikes lashed everywhere, they still looked ordered and sea-ready.

We had in common that we were in the midst of the most audacious leaps of our lives. We had finagled a stretch without the rut of routine if not without bumps; for once it was anything goes. Whereas at home we'd been regarded by family and employers as oddball dropouts, in this circle a career pause was universally considered reasonable, healthy, average. Along with our careers, we had also left behind the presumption of distance to be kept from strangers. None of us would have knocked on the door of a handsome house back home and expected a tour. Yet here we were, rowing across to pay a compliment to a neighboring boat, being invited aboard for a look and a drink, offering dinner aboard *Clarity* the next night, and another friendship might be in motion. Unlike the encounters of life ashore, these were not preordained by livelihood, social class, neighborhood, or even country of origin; we were all here for the ports of call. Perhaps because our floating neighborhood was so easy to disperse and reassemble, the risk attached to social missteps was reduced. Ashore, if that first episode with the new neighbors doesn't work out, the next day they'll still be living next door. Here all of us, even those normally the most reserved, tried out a bracing directness, and discovered the rapid closeness it fosters. Because we never knew if we would see each new crew again, there was an urgency, like at summer camp, to the life story-telling. If the spark was there, then we would adjust our itineraries to meet again. If it wasn't, we could just float away. Brian and I never announced that we were together, but the amount of first person plural in our talk and the neatly-made double berth in the forward cabin made two plus two. No one felt the need to say, "Hey, wait a second, are you . . . ?"

Nowadays we would never experience such a long stretch devoid of gay socializing. Then, we were far from being a blasé, two-part unit looking outward. For each of us, going about life as a gay man was still plenty to get used to, never mind being part of a couple. Emerging from our respective closets, we were feeling our way, without speaking about it, toward how out we were going to be, how much we were going to let the comfort of others govern our demeanor. And given the rather staid mores of the West Indies, combined with a macho culture, the comfort of others was not exactly nourishing much gay life for us to engage with. Looking back though, it was not a bad thing at that stage to be deprived of our own kind; at least it reassured us of the acceptance possible in straight circles.

One of our first mail pick-ups included a note from my mother—brief, chatty, wishing us well. The last line startled me to tears: "I'm so glad you met Brian in time to share this wonderful experience." Mild words, but to me, a bolt from the blue. So she knew who he was to me and blessed us. To this day, through countless cordial visits, that is the closest either of my parents has come to an explicit acknowledgement of us. They have chosen instead to show me, in their muted, Lutheran way, that they like, respect, and accept Brian, because our life together makes me happy. I used to assume that some day we'd need to push on to a real face-off, clear the air. But I've come to feel that would be a selfish, possibly hurtful, indulgence on my part, and yet . . . words like these on a page therefore take us into uncharted territory.

Our conversational equivalent, those floating evenings, for the cocktail party "and what do YOU do?" was "and how did YOU pull this trip off?" I was fascinated to hear the tales, to find that just behind safe picket fences in many lands were mad schemers building boats in barns, wrecking marriages, sailing huge distances on nothing but canned peas.

In Beaufort we had met the crew of a homemade steel ketch from England. To finance their trip they had scoured London for antique maps, prints, and books from around the world. In each new island or country they visited, they would go ashore with materials from that place, find a local antique shop, and deal. Years later we heard that they had been caught anchored in the crossfire of the civil war in South Yemen, had fled to the safety of a nearby ship, and from there had watched their boat—named *Innocent Bystander*—sunk by shelling.

Through that couple we had met a handsome young Frenchman named Philippe. He was crewing aboard a forty-one-foot ketch skippered by a brooding man from California whose entire family had jumped ship in the first week of his dream cruise. Philippe had sailed with his Ahab from California, through the Panama Canal, across the Caribbean, and up the U.S. East Coast. Their long upwind passage from the canal to Jamaica had included being aground for a day on submerged reefs hundreds of miles from the nearest land. When they had finally arrived in Kingston the owner refused to go ashore and insisted on leaving for Florida in the morning. At each stop thereafter, Philippe would go ashore alone; the owner would sit aboard with his back issues of *Reader's Digest* and drink warm gin. Now Philippe had come as far as the Virgins with him but was fed up. He had arranged a crew berth aboard a ketch bound for Vancouver via the Panama Canal and the Tuamotus of the South Pacific. He just needed a lift to St. Barth's to make the connection. Three weeks later we dropped him aboard *Candlewin* in Gustavia, St. Barth's. He has since married the sister of *Candlewin*'s owner; he lives in Vancouver and is building his own boat.

We met a physician who had built his ferro-cement schooner and sailed it alone from South Africa. He was traveling on a British passport, had painted "LONDON" as his hailing port on the transom, and had forged ship's papers so he could visit the many countries that wouldn't let South Africans in. We met a Dutchman who had not officially cleared into or out of a single island in a year of cruising the Caribbean. There were many Swedes, speaking their idiomatic English, learned from watching *Dallas*. Swedish income taxes are so high that a middle-income Swede can sail for half of each of two years and save enough on taxes to pay for the whole trip.

As time went on and we sailed down along the chain in our loose flotilla, these friendships, hatched in intriguing detail, deepened with shared adventures. Most of our new friends were British. South of Antigua we saw hardly any American boats. This was my first extended experience with Brits besides Brian; gradually I learned which things of his that I'd always considered idiosyncrasies were actually just Britishnesses, and vice versa. We all contributed entries to our English-American lexicon. Secure among his own, he held me up for ridicule for having corrected his pronunciation of "aluminium." He confessed to having been in North America so long that he was no longer sure which idiom was coming out when he spoke.

One day, anchoring in Martinique, we were greeted by a man from Northumberland, in northernmost England, who had seen Brian's Scottish flag flying at the spreaders. Tony Van Hee had sailed across the Atlantic with his wife, Joan; their three children, Victoria, ten, Jason, eight, and Georgina, two; and a young friend, Nick, along as crewman and tutor. We quickly hit it off.

During the next days, we explored together, shared dinners and sunsets. Vicky and Jason took our sailing dinghy on tradewind voyages to shore, where they would solemnly anchor it as though it were a tea clipper, and wade ashore to practice their correspondence school French on the shop-keeper. Tony worked at building the kids their own sailing dinghy. His work-shop was the deck of a French boat he was looking after for the owners. More exactly he was looking after the boat's parrot, which whistled the "Marseillaise" every hour or so. These three boats were anchored close to-gether; if we needed an onion, or Tony needed an extra pair of hands, it was just a few pulls on the oars.

This was the first cruising family I had known. Tony and Joan felt their way along the line between making the kids bold in the world and protecting them from harm. One day Joan and Georgina were headed ashore when Joan found she'd forgotten her wallet. Throwing the dinghy painter care-lessly around a cleat, she climbed aboard and went below to get it. The line pulled free and Georgina started to drift downwind, toward Panama. Tony looked up from his work and saw her floating by, looking around, uncon-cerned. "Row, Georgina, row!" he exhorted her, smiling broadly. Georgina waggled the oars in the air, checking over her shoulder to make sure she had an audience. After a minute Tony dove in and swam to her rescue.

Tony was a self-made man, owner of a trucking firm. He was as bluff and upbeat as Joan was modest and low-key. He spoke in assertions: "That would be wrong though, wouldn't it." I took some time to realize that I did not have to come out for or against him at each sentence. From the start I noticed that Tony and Brian were just slightly not at ease with each other, not actually uncomfortable, but a bit alert. As we went on to meet more Brits I would see over and over what potent signals accents could be.

If I'd met Joan under different circumstances, I'd have thought she'd be the last person to end up on such a voyage. Not that she appeared discon-tented; she was sweet and patient with the kids, listening to their latest dis-coveries, asking questions, drawing connections to other places they'd been. She just never seemed to focus on the sailing part or the oddness of family life afloat. This was simply where the family was, meals would be prompt, the children would mind their manners. She tolerated Tony's man's-man manner with an amused wink our way.

Jason and Vicky were bright, vigorous kids; Georgina serenely awaited her coronation. Vicky knew every brand of boat, and after a few days, presented us with an impressively-detailed watercolor of *Clarity*. Jason interrogated me about every line and chock and liked to explore our bookshelves. When Joan and Tony corrected their manners, it was not a capturing of offspring under a thumb, but a reminder of rules to a game they all agreed had merit. Even if there were still hints in Tony of a rambunctious side that made Joan roll her eyes, he was living proof of the doors that good behavior could open. It was this coexistence of exuberance and civility that struck me as different and British.

My course in Britishness continued one evening in Rupert Bay, Dominica. One of the most splendid yachts I'd ever seen anchored next to us, a large white sloop with gleaming varnished cabin sides. She was clearly not of our ilk but I made an exception. When a distinguished-looking gentleman emerged from the forward hatch, erected a canvas deck chair and sat down with a book, I rowed over to pay my respects. His name was Tony Perry; he was the boat's professional skipper. The boat was *Djinn*, the Morgan family yacht (J. P.'s grandson was the current owner), and, as I've since learned, one of the most famous of American yachts. Tony was British, perfectly gracious; he did not invite me aboard for a look: "Perhaps another time."

The boat was run the old-fashioned way in some respects: when the Morgans were aboard, Tony was not to be aft of the mast in harbor unless invited. And since the Morgans were keen sailors, he was not to enter the cockpit under way unless invited. He later told us stories of coaching Mrs. Morgan, in her eighties, as she steered through busy English Harbor, Antigua. Her eyesight was failing, but she loved to steer. Tony would stand just outside the cockpit: "Perhaps just a bit to starboard, Madam, NOW!"

Not so traditional was the fact that Mrs. Morgan also loved to cook and always cooked for her guests. So Tony was to fix a meal for himself and the deck hand, clean up, and be out of the galley by seven, when she would take over. When the family was not aboard, Tony was free to use the boat as he wished—he later invited us aboard on many occasions—so long as he arrived at the next rendezvous.

Tony was an elegant, personable, well-read gentleman making an excellent living, responsible for a seventy-two-foot yacht of matchless pedigree—

in other words, a servant. He spoke easily of this, without a trace of apology. He was secure in his abilities, proud of his position of trust. He saw no need, as I might have, to say "I'm just doing this till I can save enough to do such and such," or to express disdain for his employers, or in any way to rebel against his station. He told us that when Sparkman and Stephens, the premier American yacht design firm, designed a boat of this size, their services sometimes included hiring a skipper for the client. Most American clients requested British skippers because their fellow Americans just did not seem to be constituted for service, whereas in Britain it is an ancient and honorable occupation. Later in the winter, when I was starting to scheme for a way to make paradise last, there was some loose talk of my hiring on as the next year's deck hand. But on reflection, I had to admit it would not be for me.

Brian began each day with a plunge into the harbor; I would put the coffee on and sit half-awake in the cockpit staring straight ahead. On our interisland hops, I wore long-sleeved white shirts and pants; Brian wore nothing. We negotiated over how much to leave the hatch open over our heads at night. Brian slept through the midnight showers; I rescued the towels from the lifelines. We settled into the patterns of our being together.

At times, as we cruised, we dared to think that, apart from the varnishing, we had life pretty well in hand. *Clarity* was tidy, no one was anchored too close, tomorrow's dinner was in the icebox, we had a spare of pancake syrup. This circumscribed world was comprehensible, manageable, less stressful even in its moments of hazard than what we all called the "real world." Occasionally, however, there were intruding reminders of beckoning complexity.

Arriving in St. Vincent, northernmost of the Grenadines, we checked at the Mariners' Inn for forwarded mail. In the stack was a frantic letter from Brian's secretary during his fellowship, telling him to call Yale immediately and act interested if he wanted a job. She had actually called the Coast Guard to see if they would find us. Brian called; he got the job. It was a relief for him to have reentry settled, but from that moment on, we stopped looking at each harbor town and saying, "This could be nice, a house right over there . . ."

Our southernmost port of call was Port of Spain, Trinidad; we had timed our visit to hit Carnival. Lifelong family friends of Brian's, the Jardines, were expecting us. We arrived bearing a four-foot wahoo we'd caught on the overnight sail from the Grenadines, sufficient for a barbecue for ten.

Brian and me in the Caribbean, 1982. At times, as we cruised, we dared to think that, apart from the varnishing, we had life pretty well in hand.

The Jardines had been in Trinidad for many generations, prosperous in shipping. Their family burial plot was in the middle of Port of Spain's main park, the Queen's Park Savannah. The family homes were in a compound high in a mountain valley. We sipped drinks under the slow fans in a vast white living room with giant, ornate Victorian furnishings. The floor of black and white marble diamonds continued through arched doors onto a terrace overlooking the city and the Gulf of Paria beyond. It was my first glimpse of the lives led in the villas we'd seen overlooking each harbor down through the islands.

The Jardines' days of joining in Carnival were over. At the end of the evening, they dropped us off back at the dinghy dock, warned us to be careful of our wallets, and promised they'd listen to our stories when it was over.

The next morning we plunged into the melee. Carnival is the central event of Trinidad: six months of stitching and rehearsing, a week of unrestrained bedlam, and six months of telling the tales. There are certain scheduled parades and competitions, but the teeming density, the exuberance and tumultuous release that swept us away were beyond the vision of organizing committees. The parades had no spectators, but were human rivers, lapping up the alleyways, rippling in time with whichever calypso or steel band held sway for that block.

The Queen of Carnival was a butterfly with a thirty-foot wingspan emblazoned with the Andy Warhol portrait of Marilyn Monroe, meticulously reproduced in sequins. The King's costume was entitled "the Sacred and the Profane." His wings were sequined rays radiating from two bodies, joined at the back. Facing front, the King wore a body-stocking, painted to accentuate his muscles. Facing rear was a limp, haggard, puffy effigy of the devil. This idolatry was a national sensation; the King strutted across the front pages for days. A country that would enshrine the male body and its sensuality as the centerpiece of its main cultural event felt like a good dream.

We jounced along for hours, every so often grabbing a shark sandwich or a roti—a tortilla wrapped around goat curry—from one of the many street stands. In one block we came upon the steel band Pandemonium putting out a blistering samba, the ranks of players prancing in place as they let rip bizarre and perfect syncopations. Throughout the tune, the crowd surged right through the middle of the band, dancing, clapping, cheering. I stood in mid-band transfixed, like a log snagged in floodwaters, tears of elation flowing, grinning, nearly levitating, the music as embracing and exalting as Beethoven's Ninth. Ten years before, at the Be-Ins in Central

Park, such scenes had only piqued my longing. Finally I could let the music in, and let my body answer it.

Each predawn, as we retreated in the dinghy to collapse aboard *Clarity,* the roar of mingled calypso followed us out across the water. Never having seen so many people so ecstatic for so long, I eagerly steeped myself in this potent emotional bath of unselfconscious mass delight.

On Ash Wednesday, after one last go-for-broke paroxysm—which featured people running through the streets daubing total strangers with chimney soot and shoe polish—the music stopped. The population stumbled home to sleep it off.

In the next days, we toured the landmarks of Brian's childhood. (I nearly got to see his childhood bedroom, but he lost his nerve when, as he was pointing it out, a maid leaned out its window and asked what we wanted.) Our guide was Ian Jardine, whom I'd met at dinner the first night—a distinguished-looking, trim bachelor in his sixties who also lived in the family compound. His home, the Hermitage, was elegant, deeply shaded, and formal, hung with his cherished collection of antique maps and prints of Trinidad. He had a broker in London who was charged with recovering as much as possible of the Trinidadiana that had been carted away in the steamer trunks of the departing British colonials when Trinidad became independent in 1962. He took us to a trusted shop and guided us through the purchase of an antique map of the West Indies.

Nothing was ever spoken about it, but I had a sense that perhaps, long ago, he had seen signs—the boy Brian quiet, not in the center but at the edges of scenes—signs familiar from his own youth; that perhaps he was gratified now to see the man Brian happy, vigorous, on an adventure. His hospitality had a paternal quality; I thought I detected in him a bittersweet pleasure in seeing the next generation living what had been so much more forbidden to his.

Finally, it was time to start back north. In Grenada, we fell in with two boatloads of bright, antic young Londoners who were, I felt, more my counterparts than the other Brits we'd met. Well, all right, so they were more prosperous than I, drastically. They were also, we found out as we got to know them, a sort of itinerant soap opera. Looking back, I realize how preposterous my notion of kinship with them was at the time, as I was lord of the biodegrading dome. The notion meant a change of course had been set in motion within me. Soon mere buckets to catch the leaks would not be enough of a solution.

We were all island-hopping northward, toward Sailing Week in English Harbor, Antigua, the last roundup of the season. Despite their lovely boats and evident breeding, this crowd's live-aboard style was more like camping out: sleeping bags and canned Spaghetti-o's. They were taken with *Clarity*'s wine glasses and paintings on the walls, and took to calling her the country cottage. As they fell in and out of love with each other and played Musical Boats, our settee became the therapy couch; on a given day's cocktail hour only certain permutations of dinghies could be tied to our transom. Our being gay set us safely apart, presumably neutral ears. There was no suggestion that it disqualified us from dispensing advice. Not to make light of it; there was genuine jilted anguish to hear of. Yet, for all the sharp wit of this circle's talk, the anguish was muted and private. Nothing could have been farther from, say, Judy Zappia's volcanic Brooklyn temperament or the astrologically-correct histrionics of my fellow flower children in Vermont.

In English Harbor we anchored in a neighborhood dense with boatloads of friends, including another sloop full of young Londoners, an Irish boat, and a large motorsailer belonging to a retired British naval officer and his wife. In the final burst of socializing, talk turned to plans for homeward voyages, and what after. We had started preparing for our own passage home. We had called England from Bequia and ordered an Aries windvane self-steering device sent to Antigua. With the help of a taxi driver who was distantly related to the Minister of Approved Undertakings, we got it through customs in just one day. We went stern-to at Nelson's Dockyard and bolted it on with the help of electricity from the motorsailer's generator. From the first trial run it has worked perfectly and steers us now across the Atlantic.

I am an eager student of accents; I feasted on the array of differing British accents on all sides. I was learning their power. I now understood why Tony Van Hee and Brian were still slightly stilted with each other: Though Brian had a middle-class upbringing, his British colonial accent sounded upper-class English; Tony's, for all his prosperity, didn't. Tony didn't often mix with the Londoners either, not quite comfortable. Strangest to me was Brian's unease at the voice of the cook on a crewed private boat nearby. She was born Polish and learned her English as a governess in an upper-crust English family. Her fluty tones coming over the radio could stop Brian in mid-sentence. While noting these anti-egalitarian symptoms, I nonetheless found the stew of British voices soothing. Perhaps I was simply a commoner from the revolted colonies, showing vestiges of loyalist tendencies, basking in the approval of the oppressors.

There was something poignant too, about Brian's face as he told new British friends he was Scottish. This would be greeted with at least an eyebrow twitch of skepticism, for his accent was certainly not Scottish, and I could see Brian wanting to, but deciding not to, explain all about his upbringing in Trinidad. That could sound defensive. What I couldn't yet fathom was the bottomless history behind his urge to claim not Britain as a whole, but Scotland, as his own.

On April 18, Brian's birthday, we had a surprise party aboard *Clarity*: Tony Perry, from *Djinn*; the Van Hee family, with a hand-painted card and gift bottle of Jura single malt Scotch whiskey; and most of the cast of the soap opera. One of them, Rupert, a young shipping broker, was freshly jilted and so heartbroken he was about to fly home to London to lick his wounds. He had anchored his boat in the inner harbor, tied to the mangrove trees. But, stiff-upper-lipped, he came to the party with his full-arm monkey puppet, who conversed extensively with the children.

A few weeks later, in late May, Brian flew back to Washington to give a research paper at the national pediatrics meetings, as though the real world were making him say the password before readmitting him. When he returned, we had a last idyll in the uninhabited Prickly Pear Cays north of Anguilla, and then set off for home.

The first leg from the Caribbean to Bermuda remains my personal benchmark for dream passages: six days of reaching, reading, cooking. The only noteworthy event was an assault by a squadron of small flying squid. Brian was hit in the side of the head, and ink spots left by the casualties were everywhere on deck. I only wish we had photographed them before we scrubbed them off, as it seems only cephalopodologists believe such creatures exist.

For the second leg, on to Newport, we were joined by Steve Levinson, my next-door neighbor from Vermont, and we discovered what a difference the luxury of a six-hour stretch of sleep at sea can make. There was some fairly brisk weather which Steve told me put dread in my eyes, and therefore in his, but we made good time and found North America despite pea soup fog.

We had gotten away with phase one of the Big Plan. Now: back to work, save some money, and start planning the main event—crossing the Atlantic.

Journal entry, July 4, our thirteenth day out: "I awake early to Bob making homefries, part of a cheddar omelet breakfast. There is still enough ice for beers, seltzer, and three-quarter-point champagne. 458 to Horta.

"Part of my transition to passage life was going from thinking of each day as a countdown unit, packed with errands, tasks, calls, lists, to this realm of nebulous clock time and the ingenuity required to divide twenty-four-hour days into satisfying blocks of reading, navigating, cooking, bathing, conversation, writing, sleeping. There is plenty to do, plenty of variety. Nonetheless, it takes a positive attitude to keep from focusing on the confinement.

"As *Clarity* reels off the hundreds and hundreds of miles, her power and ability slowly erode my deep fears: passage-making seems more and more a reasonable endeavor. I no longer awaken disoriented and panic-stricken.

"The months of preparation stoked my propensity for worry, which is basically future-oriented. On this passage I've slowly hauled my experiencing back from some calamity-ridden future to a stream of rich and benign present moments."

Shortly after I write this, Brian comes out into the cockpit where I am sitting. I show him the journal entry, the first time I've done that on the passage. He reads it, looks up smiling, and gives me a hug.

On the matter of this nebulous time: My brain is easily boggled by time zones; if it weren't for the rule Spring forward, Fall back, daylight saving time would stump me. The mere presence out there of the international date line may be the reason I have no great desire to sail in the Pacific. At the same time I consider myself a good explainer, someone able to render confusing matters—like the A-flat minor scale—comprehensible, and someone valuing that quality of expression so much that I named my boat *Clarity*. So it was out of something like a sense of *noblesse oblige* that I lay in my berth a few days ago trying to come up with the explanation to end all explanations for Bob, my trusting navigation student, of why we had to subtract from (or was it add to?) Greenwich mean time to get local time. Amid fumes of heating brain tissue, I grappled to hold in my mind an image of the earth rotating, at the same time orbiting the sun, us moving across its surface, tiny people going to bed in England. Then, as though balancing this apparatus on my head, I got up, and with much gesticulating, explained it all to him. He was confused, naturally, but by speaking more and more loudly, I finally got it through his head. When his resulting calculations put us a thousand miles from our estimated position, he and Brian ganged up on me and left me refuted, dishonored, adrift without certainties. Only by adopting the same attitude I take toward international monetary fluctuations have I been able to go on. But that's not the only mischief time is getting up to.

Since we are traveling almost exactly due east along the fortieth parallel of latitude, we are ticking off meridians of longitude, and therefore time zones, at a good clip. This has led to disintegration; time is now running on four separate tracks. First, since we can easily notice the difference in the hour of sunset from one night to the next, we keep advancing ship's time on the main bulkhead clock so that our three night watches will span the hours of darkness. Second, we're maintaining Saybrook, Connecticut, time on one wristwatch, for ease of knowing which day of the passage it is, the mileage for each twenty-four-hour period, and thus the passage totals, averages, and possible time of arrival. Third, for celestial navigation, we are keeping Greenwich mean time on two other wristwatches, checking it daily with the time beeps before the *BBC World News*. And fourth, part of the celestial navigation routine requires the reckoning—the occasion of my earlier humiliation—of local time by time zone compared with Greenwich mean time, and this official local time has not necessarily agreed with our ad hoc juggling of the bulkhead clock. All of this is not an arrangement we learned from some book.

These four concurrent versions of what time it is leave an inveterate timekeeper like me about as secure as if I were crossing a river on ice floes, but we also have present yet another effect whose influence I can only guess at. We are experiencing, over each several-day stretch, a season's worth of alteration in the schedule of light and dark. While jet lag introduces a surreal quality to perception (and thus to modern diplomacy), at least it is smoothed out once and for all in a couple of days. This is like jet lag administered by IV drip. Who knows what yo-yoing our hapless biorhythms are undergoing as the same kinds of cues that switch on the maple sugar industry each year, that make salmon head for the rivers, geese head back to Canada, are compressed from three months into three days?

Last night we were calling a passing ship when we were answered by a yacht somewhere nearby but out of sight below the horizon. It was an Italian sloop, being sailed by a delivery crew from the West Indies to Italy via the Azores. They will be staying in Horta only two days because the skipper must hurry on to Italy so he can fly back to the Caribbean to squeeze one more delivery in before the worst of hurricane season. To me this shows insufficient worry and probably no time at all for nameless dread. It is as though we're a South Pole expedition nearing its mark and encountering a mailman. We agreed to speak again but have not gotten any answer at the appointed times. Perhaps they don't know what time it is either. Bob refers to the skipper as Carmine, pictures him as a Flatbush Avenue hitter, and for some reason is convinced that there are lonely women aboard. He stands on deck scanning the horizon.

July 5, 316 miles to Horta. With so few miles to go, the mere sight of the North Atlantic chart is a boost. Its necklace of circled crosses wobbles out from under overhanging Newfoundland and ends tantalizingly close to the scattering of specks. The weather continues clear, warm, with light, intermittent breezes. We motor or sail accordingly. Daily swims are routine. Today we haul aboard a three-foot diameter Day-Glo pink plastic ball of the sort used as fenders on commercial fishing boats. Thinking to barter with the natives, we set about cleaning it up. Brian forks overboard its twitching colony of critters and we swab its painted numbers with acetone, which, while not removing the numbers, does dissolve the plastic, deflating the fender for good. Another busy hour passes at sea.

July 6, 205 miles to Horta. The abundant sea has sent us another Day-Glo pink fender, which we depopulate and hang off the transom.

July 7, 120 miles to Horta. The Azores archipelago sprawls over several hundred miles of ocean, and Flores, the westernmost island, is about a hundred miles west of all the others. It has a tiny village, no harbor—true of several of the islands—and is rarely visited by yachts. It lies about twenty-five miles north of our course. This morning, I get out the chart of the Azores for the first time. I plot our position on it and figure out the compass direction to Flores. Coming up on deck with mock ceremony, I aim the hand bearing compass in that direction and announce that there lies Flores. I am actually quite certain it is too far away to see. But where I have pointed, there does seem to be a good-sized clump of cloud, often a sign of land. Peering through the binoculars, I think I see, but no, but yes, but YES. LAND HO! Nothing more than the faintest of sloping lines, demarcating two shades of hazy blue as alike as adjacent color chips at the paint store, but unmistakable: the profile of a headland dropping out of the cloud to the horizon. Fifteen days.

We cheer, we hug, we take a futile picture. Bob is for going over just to make sure it is Flores, as a flyer might. He accepts our veto cheerfully. He is so effusive about our skill as navigators, seamen, general all-around great guys, that I have some inkling of the doubts he may resolutely have been keeping to himself. We are ecstatic for the whole day. The ice is finally gone, so the champagne is warm. For the occasion, Bob digs out his tourist t-shirt, printed with dangling cameras. Brian's a boyish impresario, composing snapshots of our toasts. Knocking on wood every few minutes, I'm beginning to dare to think this can't be taken away from us now.

During the afternoon, we see the masts of another sailboat to the south, on a similar course, converging with us on Horta. Bob hopes it's Carmine and wants to head over for liberty, but it's got three masts, Carmine has one. They don't answer our radio call. They are ghosting in the faint breeze, we are motoring, so we leave them behind.

Bob makes a special pasta dinner with a sauce of olive oil, anchovies, capers, Dijon mustard, and egg yolks, among many other things. At dinner time we reckon we have seventy-five miles to go.

The remoteness of being on the open ocean, for all its dangers, does offer guaranteed protection against what is, after all, the single greatest killer of boats besides decay and the wrecker's hammer: colliding with the earth. Part of the appeal of voyaging is the disconnectedness, the not caring where you are, closer than say, a twenty mile radius (about twelve hundred square miles), a loose luxury unthinkable any other time. At sea the fine detail of coastal piloting gives way to a grainier scale of distance and time.

At passage's end, the reverse adjustment is needed; Faial lurking just seventy-five miles away seems cause for concern. (Approaching St. Thomas in 1981, I started casting eager glances ahead when we were still 110 miles out.) Anything for a worry, some will say. Well, I'm not fretting about it, but, as we sit our night watches, we're peering strenuously ahead for the first twinkles on Faial's hillsides, listening through the clatter of the diesel for the sound of breaking waves. Returning from the Caribbean, our approach to the Rhode Island coast was shrouded in fog. At least they don't have that around here, according to the books.

On Brian's watch, the seventy-six-hundred-foot summit of the island of Pico, just beyond Faial, is briefly silhouetted in moonlight, but, strangely, there is no trace of Faial, which is closer and has a thirty-four-hundred-foot central peak. Later, on my watch, I see a light; too soon to be land. I assume it's a ship, but there is something too complicated about its appearance, too quick about its approach. Then I realize it's not a ship miles away, but a sailboat perhaps a hundred yards away, motoring in the opposite direction. Through the binoculars I can see the person at the helm and clothes hanging over the lifelines. How did they get so close without my seeing them? There are still stars overhead but, sure enough, the woolly sky-sea edge has pulled closer all around. We are motoring into a fogbank.

Gradually the stars fade, the cockpit is drenched with mist. At the slow dawn we are socked in.

We motor through the early morning, conjuring stretches of shore in the dull distance. The airport at Horta has a radio beacon. I get out the radio direction finder and pick up the signal. On the chart Brian plots the direction from the source. We determine that we can safely head for it: the radio beacon is near the coast and there is deep water in close to shore. We motor for several more hours, homing in on it, studying the gray, calling out false alarms.

Finally, over a period of several minutes, we become aware of a color in the mist that we haven't seen in sixteen days: green. Then, a stony beach, a building, white with red tile roof, cows grazing. We're about a mile off shore. The fog is burning off rapidly now in the morning sun, revealing higher and higher elevations. Lush hillside fields are divided by dark green hedgerows. There's the airport. Cars move along the roads. We're given a last pass by porpoises, turning us over to the land.

We devour these sights; the binoculars make the rounds over and over; both cameras snap away. My broad grin has lower lip tremble; behind the sunglasses, there are tears. When Brian is this happy, his pronunciation takes on a flavor—he speaks straight through the smile locked on his face—that I associate with our most exultant moments together.

Brian raises the yellow quarantine flag to the starboard spreader: the international signal requesting customs and immigration clearance on entering foreign waters. We motor past the caves on the southeast promontory, up the channel between Faial's east coast and nearby Pico. Horta appears on the port hand, an old, solid, small city—white, pastels, red tile, palms. We round the end of the massive breakwater. Small children are racing sailing dinghies. We are safe.

A forest of masts rises behind an inner breakwater which is not on our

Landfall, Faial, the Azores, after sixteen days at sea. When Brian is this happy, his
pronunciation takes on a flavor—he speaks straight through the smile locked
on his face—that I associate with our most exultant moments together.

chart, nor mentioned in our guidebook. We had expected to tie up alongside
a fishing vessel inside the old breakwater. But since the time the chart and
book were printed a couple of years ago, the Portuguese government has
built a lavish new marina, tardy recognition of Horta's long-held status as
a midocean haven for sailors.

I circle while Brian and Bob root out the fenders and dock lines, then
we head in to tie up at the customs and immigration dock. Portuguese people take our lines; they're not amazed. We step ashore: sixteen days to the
hour, 2,050 miles.

When we take our passports and ship's papers to the offices, we are told
it is time for midday closing. I'm resigning myself to cooling our heels aboard
for two hours when, in a refreshing departure from official ways the world
over, they say we're free to go up into the town for our own lunches, the
boat will be safe at the government dock, come back anytime after two.

So, minutes after touching land, we are off exploring. My sea legs are
wobbly; taking more than four steps in one direction is novel. The sidewalks
heave slowly underfoot as my body plays out its seagoing state.

Everything is sharp, fresh, not just land, but foreign land. The steep, swept streets are of small laid stone, the sidewalks the same but with inlaid white stone patterns of fleurs-de-lis, swans, breaking waves. There are flowers everywhere, a steady din of birds. The town has been here for four hundred years and has the richly, almost geologically layered quality of an old coral reef.

We're hungry, so this is not a dawdling first look. I'm greedily soaking up details, happy, agitated, as though being hurried through Christmas. Bob strides ahead to assume his role as our interpreter, asking a policeman for a restaurant recommendation. Brian, a believer in do-it-yourself exploration, checks an impulse to call him back: we're equals ashore. The sidewalks are narrow, crowded, but not hectic. We step off the curb to pass or let people pass, but no one jostles. The street scene is not high-spirited but rather calm. Many of the older women wear black. There are few tourists; the locals are not overshadowed. There is not the outward-turning presenting of the place that you sense in a place like Bermuda. This is a self-contained Portuguese place. To these people, Faial is the hub of the universe.

I'm grabbing glances in shop windows; there are pleasingly odd mixes of goods: one shop sells cases of wine and gas stoves, another has straw hats, paint, and potatoes. The buildings are well-kept, proud; many have ornate detailing—ironwork balconies, glazed tile facades, varnished door and window frames.

The restaurant is modest and busy. Waiting for a table, I observe courtship customs and family dynamics, and catch the aroma of passing stews. There is only one person sitting alone in the place. We peg him as a single-handed sailor and later turn out to be right. We are given a table by the window and by the time, many tastes and toasts later, that we leave, I am in an unusual state for dealing with officials in Portuguese.

This turns out to be easy. Generally every culture produces a quota of officious busybodies to defend its borders, but these officials are unnervingly casual. We are assigned the slip next to Carmine, who turns out to be named Francis. We introduce ourselves and talk briefly; he is working steadily on laundry, clean-up, and reprovisioning for departure the next day. There are no lonely women.

There are about a hundred sailboats in the marina, perhaps ten or fifteen of them from the States. All have sailed at least a thousand miles to get here, so there is an air of competence about the boats and crews, no floating condos. The docks are surrounded by a handsome laid-stone plaza which abuts the town square and, at one end, leads to a modern building containing laundry facilities and our next must: hot showers. As we head along the dock to the showers, we greet everyone we meet with the expansiveness that comes from bursting with pride. In this place you can't crow, "Hey, we just sailed two thousand miles," but they know that smile.

The next priority is to call our parents and Diana. We have left her with a list of people to call when she hears from us, and instructions not to even think about us, never mind worry, for three weeks, and not to raise any alarms for at least six. She is so unprepared to hear from us after sixteen days that at first she can't quite compute and half thinks we've turned around and come back.

We quickly learn that the washing machines have chronic waiting lists, so we begin laundry on deck, and quickly learn that the water is shut off at five o'clock.

We're left no choice but to have our first look at the Cafe Sport. We have been hearing about it for years; it's one of a select number of such crossroads bistros in ports of the world that sailors tell each other about.

It is small, busy, fronted with three open doorways looking across the street to the harbor and Pico beyond. Super Bock beers are forty cents. Thumbtacked on the walls and ceiling are dust-darkened t-shirts with yacht names, flags of distant nations, yacht clubs, personal burgees, boat photos autographed by crews—all mementos of the celebrations of the hundreds of boatloads of sailors who have decompressed here.

The clientele at this hour is an even mix of sailors, with our cutoff shorts and sunbleached eyebrows, and local men conferring. In the back right corner is the small bar; in the back left corner, another counter, the domain of Peter Azevedo, the proprietor. Here the sailor can pick up mail and messages held for arrival, exchange foreign currency, make overseas telephone calls (shouting over the noise), buy Cafe Sport t-shirts and hats, scrimshaw, cruising guides, or receive expert advice on local services, sights, history, and restaurants. He is a soft-spoken man of about sixty, fluent in many languages, who takes pleasure from knowing the answer, solving the problem.

We sit with our beers. More and more people come in, locals stopping in after work, sailors who've been working on their bilge pumps.

After a late-evening meal in a hot, brightly-lit family restaurant, we stroll back toward the town square. It is about eleven, pleasantly warm and calm. Opposite the Sport, a couple of hundred people are taking the air sitting on the low wall overlooking the harbor. From there on, for the three blocks to the square, the sidewalks are busy with promenaders. The square itself is humming: black-clad matriarchs gossip on the benches, orbited by little kids on bikes and skateboards; parents push strollers; teens plot and maneuver to music from many tape players. Down a short bank from the square sits the fleet, glossy in the low light. I feel us meshing with the local turnings, beginning the sampling of another way that keeps me traveling.

We leave the midnight buzz and walk out the floating dock to *Clarity*. She sits as motionless as on that morning in Saybrook. We sit for a while in the cockpit, suffused with well-being. For sixteen days we've grabbed our rations of sleep, the three of us taking turns in the same two rumpled sleeping bags in the main cabin. Now crisp, fresh sheets await in the forward cabin double berth—in a few moments the pleasure of my man stretched out beside me. Sweet reward.

Manuel Gomes, our driver, was born on Faial but spent seventeen years in Bristol, Rhode Island, molding fiberglass at Bristol Yachts. He looks like a wise guy in a beer ad, but speaks in a sweet, unaffected way about how homesick he was, how he had to come back, not just to any of the islands, but to Faial. He is certain that whatever it is that may be better about any other place on earth, he can do without it.

We are heading for the "New Land." The first sign of it is a village of stone-walled ruins, partially buried in lava ash. In the near distance stands a lighthouse, formerly marking the westernmost point of the island. In 1959, a volcano erupted one hundred yards offshore, creating the black mountain beyond the lighthouse, and incinerating the village. Still nothing grows on the new land. Film crews come looking for the moon or post-nuclear New Jersey.

Farther along the coast, we stand at the edge of bluffs hundreds of feet high, looking down through the wildflowers, thick on the nearly sheer face, to the black sand shore far below. Everywhere in the countryside, each farm field of several acres is bounded by dense windbreak hedges. This is a temperate climate; savage storms sometimes rake the islands in winter. On the hills in the northwest part, the windbreaks are ten-foot hydrangea hedges now in peak bloom, like starched pale blue ruffles. Driving along a road high above the sea, with hydrangeas spilling onto the pavement and tall Japanese cedars down each side, we meet an untended herd of Holsteins, ambling the other way.

Manuel takes us to the top of Faial's quiet central volcano. From our vantage point on the rim, the six people having a picnic twelve hundred feet down in the lush crater are white specks. In a small shrine on the rim, a woman sells fruit drinks. Manuel returns us to town.

We had expected nothing of the Azores but a place to fill the tanks and make do with what the guidebook described as limited provisions. Our stay has been so unexpectedly rich I now understand why so many of the European boats in the marina have sailed over to tie up in Horta for the whole summer. The author of our guidebook must have hit Horta in a bad mood.

After an outsider's glimpse from behind a language barrier, I won't claim to have penetrated the Portuguese character. But the You-CAN-Have-It-All attitude is decidedly lacking. Widows traditionally wear black for life. When a cruise ship line tried making this a stop, the shopkeepers stayed home till the ship left. Kids are nice to each other all around us. There is a danger of cherishing quaintness in a condescending way, but, wary of ambition as I am, I consider that these people, so many of them modest, calmly friendly, are on to something.

One night we eat at a restaurant in a small seaside village. Our companion, a guy we've just met in the marina, motions us to join him in the kitchen and taste from the pot before ordering. I assume this custom is more of this pleasant openness. When he further announces that we will carry our table outside, I hope he is enough of a regular for such highhandedness, though I know he's only been in Faial a couple of days longer than we have. I've had warning signs: he is not on speaking terms with the couple crewing on his boat, and on the way over, he told the driver to pick us up at 10:30, "German time, not Portuguese time." We are two days into a cruising acquaintanceship, and I am being reminded why some are short-lived.

His name is Bernhard, a dapper man in his fifties; his boat is across from us in the marina. He was born and raised in New Orleans and has had an American wife, an Italian wife, and now a French wife. Now living in Spain, he has a hybrid Euro-accent, frequently exclaims "voilà!" His tongue is sharp: he describes a daughter as "one of the eighty or ninety thousand assistant vice presidents of Citicorp."

By moving outside, we are now sitting on the margin of the small village square. Kids are playing in the last light, a few local people sit here and there taking the evening. One spindly girl is doing a fair amount of shrieking. I'd rather she wouldn't but it's her village. Suddenly Bernhard is up, striding over to her, shaking her: "Cut this bullshit, asshole!" Brian, Bob, and I look at each other, stunned. It is miles back to Horta, hours till the taxi returns.

Conversation limps back up to speed. Our dinner arrives: polvo, a rich octopus stew with a gravy of red wine, hot pepper, and octopus ink. A boy about seven is running a demolition derby, pushing an eerily placid one-year-old in a stroller, doing laps around our table. Bernhard shows some irritation so Brian blocks the straightaway with his chair. Powering the stroller ahead like an all-terrain vehicle, the boy detours over the concrete wellhead next to the table. Suddenly Bernhard is up again. He picks the boy up by one leg and one arm and begins thrusting him at each adult in the vicinity: "Is this asshole yours?" Fortunately for Bernhard, the people are too polite, too restrained, or too baffled to react as they well might. The boy is the son of the cook; a moment later we see him sobbing into her apron. In one more corner of the world, the locals now have a story to tell, shaking their heads, about what happens when the outsiders come.

Other social forays are less eventful. In the next slip is a quiet, rangy German who has just sailed alone twenty-six days from St. Thomas. He joins us aboard a couple of times to sample the fizzy lunch wines and multitude of sausages we are bound to try. After a few days he is joined by his girlfriend Maren, who has just taken her first flight to join Frank in Horta. The plane touched down, thought better of it, took off again, circled, and came in for a second landing. She's prone to seasickness, knows nothing of sailing, and will now sail with him to "Portugal, Spain, Gibraltar, wherever the wind blows." One day they take a ferry excursion to the island of São Jorge for the day. They take a bus around the island and arrive back after the last ferry has gone. When they ask the bus driver to recommend a place to stay, he takes them home to his family for the night. They will manage.

On the other side, where Carmine/Francis had been, we now have Al, a noisy American whose boat looks like a test rig for a marine equipment catalog. He prates about his expensively-acquired weather forecasts, beeps late into the night on his digital ham radio, keeping appointments, and re-coils in horror when we tell him we're headed for Scotland: "I never want to go anywhere where the temperature is lower than my age."

One day I spot a guy carrying a disassembled autopilot through the streets. I've seen him on the docks so I hail him. Larry is British, also a lapsed musician, who dabbles in record production just enough to keep his cruise going. Peter at the Cafe Sport has directed him to an electronics repairman. He has no windvane gear and has just hand-steered with his wife and two cats from Antigua. By the end of the day, I have taken our autopilot to the same shop. The repairman takes it and its schematic diagram without blinking.

By and large though, we don't socialize very much. We're not going to be here long. These islands are so remote that there isn't the likelihood of meeting up with anyone in the next harbor, as in the Caribbean. And for all the miles we have come, Brian and I are not yet really in the swing of cruising life. We're still at mainland inhibition levels.

It's said to be bad luck to set off from Horta without painting your boat's name on the harbor wall. We knew this and brought small cans of paint in *Clarity*'s colors. When the new marina was constructed, the design included thousands of square feet of bare concrete which the sailors have already nearly covered. Some boats evidently hire on artists for the voyage, judging from the seascapes, ship- and self-portraits, trendy graphics, cartoons, and elaborate logos to be found along the wall. We claim our spot, and on and off over a period of three days, I complete a design which makes up in neatness what it may lack in flair. While I'm working, a couple of teenage boys stroll by with a soccer ball. They're Americans, of Azorean descent, here from New Bedford, Massachusetts, for their third summer visiting their godfather. They tell me that the only place in the States with direct flights to Horta is Providence, Rhode Island, because so many in that area are descended from the Azoreans who shipped aboard whalers that stopped here.

One day Brian and I take a walk to the end of the outer seawall. On the way along the quay we pass some of the large fishing boats. Aboard one, men are standing shin-deep in sardines, slicing them into bite-sized steaks and packing them in salt. On another, they are sorting larger fish by species, discarding the moray eels. On the quay, men work in pairs, untangling long fishing lines with hundreds of hooks and coiling them into small square baskets.

We've come out to the seawall to see the first generation of boat name paintings. These have a more archaeological feel than the grabby graphics on the new marina walls. Here hundreds of feet of wall are layered with faded, peeling names, under a patina of commercial harbor grime. You feel that with patience and solvents, you might uncover *Pinta*. Mostly the designs are small, sober, and quiet. When these were done, there were not hundreds of boats crossing the ocean each summer. Unlike those cartoonists on the inner wall, doodling about how much the ship's cat loved Spam, these have more the spirit of the lone hiker who places his stone on a Scottish mountaintop cairn. We find a couple of names painted by British friends of ours on their way home from the Caribbean six years earlier. On a part of the wall in behind stacked, rusting shipping containers, we come upon a freshly-painted black crest on a white field, dated some years earlier, for the sail training ship *Marques*. Underneath it, lettered on a black field: "May she and the nineteen who went down with her rest in peace." This is followed by the date of her sinking, June 3, 1984, on a race from Bermuda to New York, and then: "Retouched, June 1988."

I am much affected by this, not only by the sad event recalled, or by this anonymous gesture of commemoration, but in another, closer way. Thoughts of our upcoming second leg have ever so lightly haunted my time here; this brings on a sudden crescendo. People do die out there. There have been other reminders. There were two dismasted boats here when we arrived and another, a Yugoslavian boat, motored in a couple of days later. After losing their rig, they had jury-rigged an antenna and had radioed a passing ship, which had dropped a barrel half full of fuel over the side for them to retrieve. Our neighbor with the beeping ham radio reported contact with a friend who hit a gale off Ireland. But the procession of perfect days here has held my worries at a distance. This quiet memorial brings into focus the next leg of our crapshoot.

We had planned to stay a week, and now preparations for Friday's departure begin to nibble at the lounging and exploring. Each afternoon we stop at the harbormaster's building. Posted on the wall is a weather map of the North Atlantic, updated daily. On Tuesday, an oblong high pressure system sprawls from the Azores to Scotland, not a single isobar (and thus no wind) between Horta and Glasgow. Our approach to Horta was in flat calm; it's been calm for days; it's not hard to picture motoring all the way, and we can't carry enough fuel for that. But things will change by Friday. We stick to our plan. So far I can't bring myself to tell Brian it's bad luck to head to sea on a Friday.

The electronics repairman now becomes our next stop each day. He remains genial; he'll get to our autopilot very soon. Yes, he realizes we're leaving Friday. After that it's on to the Sport for a couple of Super Bocks, and then to the showers before they turn the water off.

The two attendants at the showers are the only two people I've met here who have the same sullen, used-up quality as the tourist servers of St. Thomas. I think the reason in this case is the water issue, but in a larger sense the issue is always the same. This is merely one example of the perils for the community going after the tourist dollar.

When we checked in, the officials told us proudly that we could use as much water as we wanted for free. We have since learned, talking to local people, that this exquisite weather is even better than usual; with no rain water supplies are low; the marina gets priority over the town for water; restaurants are hauling water in buckets for dishwashing; there is grumbling. The shower attendants are the only steady touchpoint between Us and Them on this issue: They may have families at home dipping the supper soup water out of a hoarded bathtubful while yachties are heedlessly washing down their boats, leaving hoses running into the harbor while they stand chatting, or yodeling for a half hour in the shower. The attendants are responsible for turning the marina water on and off as instructed by city hall, and they hear from the sailors when the hoses go flaccid. So, you put your shower money on the counter, they give you a towel, you linger expectantly, and without looking up, they relinquish the teaspoon-size bar of soap. They think that the price their island has paid to lure us is too high, and they are right. Speaking as one of those lured, I'd sooner return for the prevailing generous, easygoing spirit we've found here than for the free tap water. I feel like running to city hall and saying, Stop, don't do this.

We have settled on a favorite restaurant for most evenings, with outside tables overlooking small fishing boats at their moorings. Here we can get fresh barbecued squid with potatoes, vegetables, salad, wine, and dessert, for about eight dollars a person. The cook is a scholarly, preoccupied man who steadily stokes and pokes at his fire of ages and pushes his glasses back up the sweaty, slippery slope of his nose after smashing each head of garlic with his mallet. When I tell his wife he is an artiste of the barbecue she snorts, "Artiste? That's not what I call him when I get him home."

On Thursday a boat from Camden, Maine, leaves for Ireland. We've chatted on the dock and in the Sport. The owners are a couple in their sixties, she peppery and vivacious, he looking with Yankee suspicion on all this balminess and languor. They have three younger friends crewing. They will be flying home upon arrival in Ireland, leaving the boat for next summer's cruise of the Irish west coast. They are one of the few boats heading the way we are, to where summers are short; their departure exerts a strong tug on the three of us. Do we go tomorrow?

The weather map looks much the same as on Tuesday: A large high pressure, fair weather system stretches from here to the British Isles. That must just be the average picture, I conclude hopefully. There is a fairly deep low forming near Iceland and heading east, but that will be long past by the time we could get there. And that's good because it will take care of the average two days a month of gale conditions reported for that area on our Pilot Charts. These are weather reference tools which divide the North Atlantic into squares a couple of hundred miles on a side. In the center of each square is a bristling hieroglyph called a windrose, with symbols indicating the prevailing strength and direction of local winds and currents, as well as the frequency of fog, calms, gales, high waves, and cloud cover, all based on countless ships' observations from logbooks dating back a hundred years. There is a separate map for each month, and June and July are the clear winners for what we're doing.

I lobby gently for waiting another day, without mentioning my superstition. Brian says, "I've talked to a couple of people who were shocked that we were leaving on a Friday. Seems it's bad luck. Had you heard?" "Well, since you mention it . . ." So it's decided: We'll leave Saturday.

The rest of Thursday is taken up with the repairman stop ("Soon, soon"), the nonperishable provisioning, including various pepper sauces in genteel, ornate bottles, and hauling to the boat a case of beer and three cases of pleasant, cheap table wine, which Brian warns will be scarce in Scotland.

Friday we take our heavy canvas bags to the fish processing plant, where we have cultivated a contact. He takes us to a room full of shaved ice and fills all the bags with a shovel. They're not set up to charge for such a small amount. In the afternoon we go to the marketplace for apples, oranges, bananas, plums, tomatoes, lettuce, beans, carrots, cabbage, potatoes, and cheeses—all local produce.

Back to the repairman. I've been gradually writing off the autopilot, but he's working on it when we arrive. He's glad to see us because he wants to know what the three knobs on the control panel do. He is intelligent and speaks English fairly well. But in the first place, I had hoped that, having the schematic diagram, he would not need to understand the function, but only the specifications of each component. Second, the controls are marked Trim, Rudder, and Yaw, and even the owner's manual has some trouble putting into words their exact purposes. My pidgin-mime evocation of a boat yawing brings a smile to his face but no light of understanding to his eyes. And he is doubtful that anyone on the island stocks these transistors. He remains cheerful; maybe it will be something simple.

Saturday morning there is a slight breeze. We pick up fresh bread and rolls, frozen chicken, pork, and beef. We top off the water tanks and jugs. We present the found Day-Glo pink fender to a French crew heading for the Mediterranean; they will use it when they go stern-to in St. Tropez.

A last visit to the repairman. It was not something simple, and sure enough, the repairman couldn't get replacement parts. Repair strategy has been rendered moot in any case by the fact that, to get the unit apart, he has hacksawed off the three control knobs at the stumps. I take back the body with a wan smile: I didn't have high hopes for this guy, but now the thing is worse off than ever. I'm not going to let this tarnish Horta though, the thing's always been a lemon, anyway.

We back out of our slip and head over to the government dock for fuel and official clearance. The momentousness of *Clarity* back in motion is lessened by the context: for eight days we've gotten used to glancing up to see people beginning or ending passages, with a fair amount of nonchalant posturing all around. We're all business, wistful business.

At 1330 hours, Saturday, July 16, we clear the breakwater, bound for Scotland.

As a harbor home, *Clarity* is so comfortable I forget she's an ocean-going yacht. On a harbor morning, we lounge with coffee in the cockpit (a friend calls it the porch), our hands idly playing over winches designed for thousand-pound loads. Evenings we sit sipping in the main cabin in the glow of the lamps, Schubert playing, as eleven taut stainless steel cables attempt to crush the hull or launch the mast downward like a crossbow. We move through her compact interior, turning sideways when passing each other. After a few level days, we become acclimated enough to leave a glass of water standing on a counter overnight, to leave a book opened face down on a settee.

Now, outside Horta's breakwater, I first feel her busied with the splat and slap of the small waves bouncing among the islands, feel her slowly rising and falling to the underlying long ocean swell, and I'm exhilarated by this, her other, her true identity. We motor clear of Faial's wind shadow and pick up a light westerly wind. With the diesel off, we settle into the gurgle, slurp, gush, and hiss of her easy reaching along. As she heels to her sailing posture, we adjust to slinging ourselves from handhold to handhold through the cabin, hoisting ourselves out of the downhill berth, hanging on to the door-frame while sitting on the head, bracing a foot against the chart table while cooking, never setting anything down without chocking it. All this is very good for fitness, but I must guard against growing grumpy at the effort required for the smallest task. With the finesse of a New York City bus driver, Murphy provides a lurch just as you are balanced on one foot, pulling a sock on, or transferring a cutting board full of chopped onions to the pot.

Faial and Pico recede into the haze; we pass the end of São Jorge and approach Graciosa, our last land, in late sun. As Graciosa is abeam, kitchen lights click on here and there: people starting to prepare the evening meal, people who may have no interest in ever journeying even to Faial. I peer through the binoculars at the small town on the north shore; it's not really protected enough to be called a harbor—just home to a few fishing boats.

Departure from Horta for the second and final leg, the one where we expect the worst weather. We've been joking nervously about that, recording our tans on film. I find myself furtively touching wood, like sneaking a touch of thigh at the movies.

Muted self-preservationist thoughts trudge across my mind: we could go in there, anchor for the night, put this off a day. . . .

No, this is good, right, the weather's good, I'm used to living aboard now, maybe I won't get sick. We have done the longer of the two legs—2,050 miles compared to about 1,400—and this leg doesn't end at some midocean outpost. When this one is over we've really done it.

On the other hand, while the first leg may have been the longer, it was also the sunnier, the warmer, the calmer. We've all been joking nervously about that, recording our tans on film, hoping, by our earnest acknowledgement of our good luck so far, to sweet-talk Whomever into granting us some more. I find myself furtively touching wood, like sneaking a touch of thigh at the movies, and when anyone sneezes, saying, Bless you.

A powerful schooner, everything flying, booms down past us from the north. They'll motor into Horta in darkness, excitedly sorting out the car lights, streetlights, navigation lights. Of course, I think, this is a thoroughfare, from here to Europe we'll probably be seeing sailboats all along the way.

Our plan is to sail the rhumb line to the upper left hand corner of Ireland, passing close enough to see it, then over the top, past Northern Ireland, and eastward into the Firth of Clyde on the Scottish west coast. It would be nice to cruise the Irish coast on the way by, but the extremely short summer demands that we choose one or the other, and this is Brian's homecoming voyage. We select a clean point, Achill Head, poking well proud of the Irish coast, and enter its latitude and longitude coordinates into the Loran receiver, which calculates the distance: 1,183 miles. We've measured the part from there to the River Clyde at about 260 miles.

The Loran display is flashing all the time, warning of weak signals. Since we left Connecticut, the machine, automatically comparing the quality of all incoming signals, has switched over from a chain of transmitters arrayed in Newfoundland and Greenland to a chain arrayed in Iceland and Norway. We are headed directly toward these now, so the signal strength should improve steadily. But we are also heading into a more frequently overcast part of the world; it remains to be seen what the net effect will be.

On the third day we are beating in moderate winds. I've been feeling fine. For the first time, the breeze is chilly; occasional dollops of spray reach the cockpit. Brian fights the inevitable, wearing a foul-weather jacket and swim trunks. The Loran is still flashing; we're getting mildly interested in confirming our position; the sky is clear, so we take sextant sights, taking for granted that we'll be able to do this any time we feel like it. Achill Head, 1,028 miles. At sunset, an edge of unbroken cloud cover like dented armor plate advances over us: the curtain coming down on the Azores High.

On the fourth day, still under gray skies, the Loran stops flashing. It's happy with its signals. During all the years I refused to get a Loran receiver, I lectured my sailing friends on the dangers of growing too dependent on electronics for navigation. But it is comforting, I must admit, on a day when the sun does not so much as peek out for a sextant sight, to feel we're under the informative umbrella of the Loran system.

My resistance to Loran was based on a pre-silicon-chip baby's gut feeling that capabilities so astounding could not possibly be reliable. I don't expect my nonsailing friends even to believe me when I tell them what the Loran is doing. It is picking up patterned radio pulses from a chain of precisely synchronized transmitters hundreds of miles away and calculating the difference between the original pattern, factory-programmed in its memory, and the received pattern. Using those time differences and the known speed of radio wave travel, it triangulates the set's location to within a few hundred feet, or even closer if the set is returning to a previously logged position, say a favorite fishing hole. I could go into more detail but I see the ice around me beginning to craze already. Loran is intended for coastal navigation, so its somewhat wobbly but basically accurate performance on this passage has not been a disappointment but an unexpected bonus. In addition to its position-finding function, it also comprises a navigation computer which can tell you your speed, course, distance, and bearing to any point on earth, how far you are off course, and other smart-aleck tidbits. All for $600 and the size of a box of noodles. Yet the New Haven traffic lights still can't be synchronized.

For the next two days we reach at good speed under gray skies. We're all happy to be racking up the miles: log entries in all three handwritings show each of us asking the Loran every few hours, How far to Achill Head? But in the eagerness there is a certain apprehension, a sense that each easy mile is one we're getting away with, the way you feel when you're humming down the highway with full knowledge that you're headed for a traffic jam.

On July 20, Brian notes in the log: "We have been away four weeks today." How often I've ground through four weeks without noticing its passing, lacking any reply to, What's new with you? Time seems elastic, stretching to contain the eventful periods. As for this second leg, I see it through the lens of my superstitious fear of being presumptuous about its success, so for now it must have no estimated duration. I regard the interval between now and the next safe harbor the way I used to regard an upcoming major exam or important musical performance, giving myself pep talks: Come on, do you actually think you may be approaching a calamity that you will never forget? Of course not, don't be silly. Brian already has appointments scheduled for his return to work in September. I wonder how many such arrows it would take—carrying threads across the gulf yawning before us, attaching us to the future—to form a safety net under us.

The different slants on a given time's passing struck me when we returned from our first year of cruising in 1982. I had removed myself from the day-to-day of my friends and home; the scene on my return was the next frame of a time-lapse photo sequence. One friend was still complaining about her boyfriend, but still with him; another had found Mr. Right, was married and pregnant. One, a songwriter, was still saying he had "a few things starting to happen," while another had started a business with three employees and customers on a waiting list. The next door neighbors' son had turned from a baby into a kid. The elm tree down in the meadow in front of the dome continued its ten-year dying, still managing a few sprigs of green.

After that first voyage, Brian settled into his first real job, as an assistant professor of pediatrics at Yale. Now, as he's sailing home to Scotland, he's bound to be questioning, comparing: How might things have turned out?

The first order of business at his new job was to write a research proposal to secure grant money to cover his salary. Keeping ahead of this became a constant fact of life. Those first studies looked at psychological and social aspects of childhood illness: colic, feeding problems, mothers' perceptions of their children's vulnerability and the effects of those perceptions on the children's lives. In his clinical work, besides these sorts of problems, he began to take on stubborn, time-consuming cases of psychosomatic illnesses or eating disorders—from anorexia and bulimia to extreme obesity—drawn by a fascination with the fractious power-sharing of mind and body.

It was clear from the start that Brian had a natural rapport with the mothers and kids he looked after, mostly black, mostly poor. I thought his British accent would be an obstacle, would sound too snooty, but that's never been the case. Maybe it's because he grew up in Trinidad; he seems genuinely at ease, respectful but firm, and the families respond to him in a way that says he is the first doctor they have ever felt was interested in their lives.

Both Brian and I were perfectly accepting of the return ashore. Knowing all along that the Caribbean trip would be a year, we had set our timers for reentry. In typical stoic fashion, Brian permitted himself no malaise. My settling back into teaching went less well. Aside from the issue of turning from delicious hedonism to gainful employment, there were other ways in which the shift was tricky.

The trend of the Johnson State College music department unto death had accelerated in my absence. Though still offering a bachelor of music degree, the department was down to two and a half faculty. Orders had gone out from the administration to the admissions office to stop recruiting music students. The college had unveiled its new Hospitality Services degree, preparing students to work in Stowe motels. My Jazz Ensemble, formerly eighteen players, was down to seven (if you counted the baritone sax player, a classical guitar player who had started sax lessons to help me out).

This climate had been endurable when I could say, "Well, it's just a while now till we go." But after having such an invigorating year, returning to the deathwatch was intolerable. The year had been spent taking the reins of our lives; this was drifting toward the waterfall in someone else's boat. As a purgative, I started writing a novel about a college collapsing. My lower back went out.

The dome had continued its return to the earth. A particularly vicious frost heave had split the foam wall in one place—my tenants had stuffed the crack with rags—and another couple of floor timbers had snapped. The new terrain meant the drain was no longer at the low end of the bathtub.

Clarity's return to Lake Champlain had been triumphant. Anchored in Burlington Harbor, flying a hoist of all the flags of all the countries we'd visited, she floated low under the press of dozens of friends. But I soon grew restless in the home waters. Part of the thrill of salt water sailing is the sense that the water under you is connected to all the oceans of the world. The lake, scene of my first years of cruising, seemed on my return an unconnected puddle, and the anchorages I'd learned on were jammed with sailing boomers.

Not to sound sour; Vermont had been my richest soil. But in the whirl of preparations for leaving, I had, without thinking about it, disengaged myself from my life there, let things slide. I'd secured the leaves of absence and such, the mechanisms of return, in an orderly fashion, but deeper down I was leaving for good. I didn't quite realize this until I got back, when my instincts told me that after a year, you can't just resume being resigned to things like massive leaks and blizzarded outhouse trips, burst pipes and arctic car troubles. After a year, you can't just go home.

There was another thing. When I'd left, I hadn't dared assume that the experiment of living with Brian would lead where I hoped. But, after a year on the boat, it was clear we couldn't just go back to commuting 285 miles each way for visits. A couple of weeks before Christmas, I visited him; we got a Christmas tree and decorated it. Two weeks later, he yanked the cord out of the wall, threw a blanket around the whole thing, tinsel, cranberries, and all, and stuffed it in the back of his car to head for the dome. It was time. Whatever the merits of distance in the early stages, now we belonged together.

When school got out in the spring of 1983, I moved into Brian's lakeside house in Guilford, Connecticut. As I had at other crossroads, I made this decision based on where I wanted to be, with no thought given to what I might be doing for a living. Mainly, we brought our life ashore. In place of squalls and jagged ledges, the hazards now lay in the need to fill the post-adventure void with something besides minor turf tiffs and treacherous smooth routine.

Clarity had been my turf, though I'm sure my utter graciousness had made that barely noticeable. Now we were settling down on Brian's turf, despite his being nearly three years younger than me and disinclined to bow to my greater experience and, let's face it, wisdom. It was also on my mind that, although he, from the earliest dome visits, had always accepted my ambition-free outlook, we had never actually lived together with him backing out the driveway to work each morning while I stirred my second cup of coffee and began shaping the next daylong improvisation.

I mused over the arguments I would marshal when the confrontation came: I was a deadbeat when you found me and I never promised I'd change. Ann Landers says you should never hook up with someone if you think you're going to change him. I can happily go back, anytime, to just the way I was, and so on. That first year I finished the novel, commuted to play in the Vermont Symphony, did some freelance writing, cooked and cleaned. The confrontation never came—good thing, too, because of course, that last argument had already become a lie.

A new neighbor moved in. Diana was a refugee from New York fleeing her role as de facto couples therapist for her boss and his boyfriend. She burst out laughing when she came over to introduce herself and found us having a drink, watching the sun set over the lake. "I can't believe it's starting all over," she groaned. Housefuls of her friends—many of them gay—began arriving nearly every weekend. Her boyfriend, still based in New York, was an avid sailor, and through him, the sailing bug had bitten her childhood friend Bob, who now stands his watches with us on this voyage.

The lake froze and we decided to have a skating party—roasted chestnuts, mulled wine, a bonfire by the water—the boys kept switching off our Strauss waltzes and putting on disco. Diana's kitchen and ours were going on all burners. The mysterious hatching of neighborhood.

In August 1984 we visited Britain, my first time: the Auntie Tour, two weeks, nine households. We would be greeted and shown to the guest room, which, in a few of the homes, was a long-stalled decorating project that had been hurried to completion for our arrival. Over the next day or two, without speaking about it, our hosts would come to understand, as much as they were able, that I was not just some guy Brian was on holiday with. In every case, I was made to feel welcome, Brian's contentment was noted, and we were ordered to return soon. Before we even got home, Brian's parents were getting phone calls: "It was so good to see Brian, and his friend Bill. He seems so happy! You must be very pleased." And with that, the great British burden of What will people think? began to lift from his mother's shoulders, and she and I entered onto what has turned out to be a permanent thaw.

Along with the inrush of first impressions of countryside, family, foreign ways, there was another thread that ran through the trip. Brian had been at his work in the States for a while; now he would see what paths his medical classmates had followed.

As a result of moving in with him, I had been getting a crash course in the American way of health care, as described by an often frustrated foreigner. We had talked often about the inconsistencies of the U.S. approach, where in general one's health care quality seemed wrongly linked to income, yet where New Haven welfare mothers and their children were routinely referred to Yale specialists; where a middle-class family could lose savings, home, everything, to the costs of one catastrophic illness, yet abandoned babies lived for months on hospital wards. So I was interested to see firsthand the British National Health Service, which Brian, and many Americans, feel is a better way. All health care is free for life.

We spent a day with a medical school classmate of Brian's, a general practitioner whose wife was a radiologist. The historic miner's strike was on and David was bitter: "So they're closing some mines, so what. They're offering them all jobs at other mines. The miners just won't move. They're striking over their God-given right to live in the same village as their grandfathers. This is the 1980s. I've chased all over Britain for each next rung of the National Health Service ladder, pulling the boys out of schools, away from friends, moving out of one house, into another, losing money on each one because I couldn't wait, Joan trailing along, looking after the boys, no hope of her finding a job where I do, and all for the ultimate prize of maybe £15,000 a year. These miners have to wake up."

We visited Brian's medical school roommate, a G.P. in a small Scottish west coast village where his father had been G.P. before him. Iain's practice had its color: a late-night boat rush to the bedside of a dying islander, kitchen table therapy/gossip with an ancient sheep herder, who might offer a wee dram. Iain's wife Winnie took care of their four kids and covered the practice's phone. Phone coverage had to be maintained twenty-four hours, seven days a week. Their NHS-owned house, next to the surgery, came with the practice as an inducement to a G.P. to work in so remote an area. Iain's parents still lived in the town; Iain would certainly remain there as long as his parents were alive.

G.P.'s were the mainstays of the system. There was no such thing as the small-town pediatrician. In fact, hardly any specialists of any kind practiced outside of the regional hospitals and urban centers. There were relatively few opportunities for physicians to pursue their own particular medical interests. Modest pay had long been the rule: medicine, at least in the NHS, is not a road to prosperity, but just another part of the civil service. Doctors were not perceived as a well-to-do elite, which removed at least that gulf between the doctor and the low-income patient.

I came away with more questions than answers, knowing I'd just glimpsed a corner of a big picture. But the idea of health care as a right of citizenship rang true. Brian came away as convinced as ever of that, but also with the feeling that the monolithic bureaucracy of the NHS tended to discourage the individual focus that had given spice to his U.S. career, focus that can produce real medical breakthroughs.

Back at home the manuscript of my novel was collecting a file of polite "no" letters, and I was finding the novelist/houseboy role increasingly uncomfortable. Time to get a job.

Every so often the episodic life catches up with me and I realize that while I've been doing a little of this, a little of that, people my age are becoming billionaires, recording benchmark ten-CD sets of the Beethoven sonatas, writing books that outrage the entire Muslim world, getting elected President. And here I was, one more episode—twelve years in Vermont—ended, and another—who knows what—getting under way. I didn't yet realize I was also in the midst of jettisoning my career in music. Despite all this, my job search didn't feel like a search for the next episode, but rather a search for something to fill the time until we sailed across the Atlantic. The voyage had assumed the importance of a line of demarcation in my life.

I took a job writing documentary film proposals for a small production company imbedded like a tick in the hide of Yale. There I set happily to work on an account of the American Revolution from the Loyalist perspective. I was aware that the organization had not made a film in years, but I would change all that.

Meanwhile Brian's work was shifting; the course of public events seemed to him to be taking away the luxury of choice of interests. He was impelled inexorably to research and clinical work in AIDS.

In New Haven in the mid-1980s, AIDS was a disease not just of adults, but, in heartbreaking numbers, of children too, children from families scarred with unimaginable grief, fathers gone or dead, mothers sick, surviving children losing their sisters and brothers. Brian came home with stories of great heroism and dignity, of uncles, grandmothers, foster parents, doing the decent thing, doing what had to be done; stories of great sorrow, of mothers hoping to live long enough to bury their kids.

He worked on getting kids with AIDS back into New Haven's schools, trying to shed light, rather than more heat, on this profound, fiercely debated issue, at the same time becoming both repelled by and obsessed with the labyrinthine tactical maneuvering. This fight, as well as related efforts involving foster care, housing, family support programs, drug and AIDS education programs, and so on, have moved Brian more and more into the realms of public health and social policy. The urgency of the epidemic has made it seem common sense that he work in the ways that could make the biggest difference.

In this new context, the really important things—leisure, the next big sailing venture—took on a different light. He understood the danger of burnout—saw it all around him. He remained determined to make sure he had an invigorating life outside medicine, to avoid becoming another Doctor Drudge. But it was hard to see a good point at which to take a recess from the snowballing epidemic.

At that point our next sailing plan had vaguely taken shape as another yearlong cruise: across to Scotland, a loop through the Mediterranean, a trade-winds passage back across to the Caribbean, and then home. This plan did pose a problem. Brian's first year off for cruising had been fairly acceptable in his intensely competitive world, a forgivable recharging between fellowship and job. But this second yearlong holiday could well be regarded as unseemly truancy by those stern perusers of résumés he might encounter down the road.

There was another problem with the one-year cruise plan: what to do during the winter portion. We fiddled with possible itineraries. On the earlier trip the winter had been spent in the tropics; to get to the tropics by wintertime on this trip would mean a headlong dash missing much of what we were going for. Besides, that would mean that half of the precious year, pried free at such cost, would be spent sailing through the Caribbean once again— pleasant but squandering. Gradually, the answer to both professional and climate problems became clear: we would do the trip in summer segments, storing *Clarity* along the way. How Brian might continue to get big chunks of each summer off is a question we have simply dodged: too far in the future to settle.

We hit on a tentative departure date a couple of years in advance; it was then that I experienced my first ambivalence about the undertaking. For twenty years I'd been yapping and straining at my leash, defining myself by this dream. Now the leash had been unhooked, that big German shepherd the Atlantic Ocean was sniffing me. On our sedate weekend cruises, I had always felt a romantic tug when, surveying the evening harbor, I'd see a boat getting up sail to head out into the darkness. Now the tug became a shiver.

Nonetheless, I propelled myself into the preparations, awakening my dormant list-making tendencies. I divided the projects into this year and next year; ordered a new jib; undertook some long-deferred refurbishments: new topsides paint, new cushions. I pictured her in a Scottish fishing village, on a French canal. I plunged into the catalogs, rethinking plumbing and rigging details, feeling for where to draw the line on spares, putting one foot after the other, outwardly certain. A brash, invincible, ignorant twenty-year-old had thought up this stunt. Brian and I selected a survival raft, joked bravely with the salesman about how many parachute flares, rescue strobe lights, puncture repair kits we should carry. We drafted wills. I started having dreams: *Clarity* being hauled up the first long slope of a roller coaster; *Clarity* sailing away, leaving me flailing in the water. I put in a stereo system, pictured her stern-to in Mykonos.

With 1988, the year of departure, came the time to order charts, tide tables for British waters, cruising guides to the Outer Hebrides. I pictured her sailing into Iain and Winnie's village. But life in Connecticut was so comfortable. Our cruising had lost its raw newness, had become competent, conservative, revisiting, and exploring further, known favorite waters: Maine, Buzzards Bay. The little voice whispered: Sit back, relax, what do you need this ocean-crossing aggravation for?

These internal arguments were waged from decidedly fringe perspectives. On the one hand, I was countering my doubts by burnishing the endeavor as the fulfilling of a holy obligation to myself, the honoring of a vigorous resolve of my youth, the coming through on a promise I'd made to myself twenty years earlier; whereas solid citizens would see it, apart from the lunatic riskiness of it, as a flippant shirking of all the responsibilities of adulthood, the kind of dream one should hope to outgrow.

On the other hand, while a sensible person accepts, even welcomes, a settling into home—the spruce taller, the daffodils multiplying each year—

I regarded the power that this comfy life had over me as a sinister warning sign of the end of the road, of an insidious slackening of purpose, momentum, vitality, anticipation. Mortality was on my mind: a close friend had come down with his first AIDS-related illness. For the first time I would know a friend through the capricious decline, with its cruel allotments of good health. Along with the sadness, it brought home to me that life should not be lived as though you have all the time in the world.

In talking to friends, I didn't wax rhapsodic about seeking a cosmic oneness with the sea. It's an eye-glazing topic, first of all, but also I wanted to avoid the sort of loyal but diagnostic looks it might engender. Rather I described the crossing as a necessary evil to get the boat to Europe so we could cruise there. This was reassuringly pragmatic, earthbound, and, just then, a truer reading of my own outlook.

In the spring of 1988, I quit my job (still no films made), took *Clarity*'s winter canvas off, and set to work down the final list. At this point we'd been storing her in the same boatyard for four winters; I'd gotten to know some of the yard staff, but none of the other boat owners. This spring I was newly expansive, inclined to chat up fellow laborers on, of course, selected genuine boats. After a suitable interval, say three minutes, and with the air of someone who is about to drop a name but truly wishes no hitch in the conversation, I would mention our plans. As a result, I discovered what I didn't quite know I'd been needing: a circle of people who thought it was a perfectly natural thing to do, who egged me on, who talked about the nuts and bolts of it so I could make the prospect solid, who'd already done it themselves.

There was a shy man in his sixties, who had built his thirty-five-footer and sailed with his wife to Portugal, the Caribbean, Bermuda. His wife had now been dead for some years; gradually he had adapted the boat for sailing alone.

One of the guys on the yard crew lived on his boat with his wife, a nurse, and their two-year-old son. They were methodically laying the groundwork for a major cruise, still a few years off, renovating two properties for rental to provide income, and waiting for their son to be old enough to remember it.

There was an elderly man, Paul Schimert, originally from Germany, who had taken up sailing late in life. A retired orthopedic surgeon, he clambered happily over his forty-footer, as intent as if she were a gratifyingly fractured patient, devising meticulous projects robust enough for rounding the Horn. His wife hated sailing. He'd tried to win her over with light weather runs, short hops, perfect reaches, all in vain: she was either bored or terrified. Still, the boat was his great passion; he lived for the tinkering and for each summer's cruise with his two elderly brothers. Though he acknowledged that I was more experienced than he—he'd read some of my sailing articles—he spoke to me about my preparations in an ardent, lecturing way, which I accepted as a sign of how much he wished he were doing it.

And there was Barry White, working calmly and competently to restore the grand, sixty-year-old, sixty-foot cabin cruiser *Annie Laurie*. After my opening gambit he generously acted impressed and allowed that he had formerly been a sailor himself. It was only in subsequent conversations that I dragged out of him that in the late 1960s he had taken his family cruising for five years in the South Pacific. The nurse I mentioned above I now learned was his daughter. Over beers after a day's sanding, he stirred his memory, lamenting that the stories were all gone, then managing to retrieve a few, then a few more, which he told with such simple relish they sounded never-before-told, yet with such a distant gaze I knew they had to be as polished as beach stones. The stories made me burn to go everywhere, life was so short.

A few weeks before we set off, my father sent me a clipping from the *Ithaca Journal* about a crew from a town near Ithaca who were heading off on a similar passage. A week or so later he sent another clipping about that crew encountering thirty to thirty-five knot winds and steep seas, experiencing a rapid collapse of morale, aborting the passage, diverting to Bermuda, flying home with no further sailing plans. In his usual laconic fashion my father commented: "I trust you are better prepared."

We had a bon voyage party about a week before departure. *Clarity* had been launched and was tied up in a slip. The stereo was firm, the decks littered with unsalty-looking people taking the hot summer evening air. I was below, happily tending bar, somewhat the worse for wear, when I heard there was someone to see me. I went up the companionway to find Paul Schimert, in a suit and tie, proffering two bottles of German wine. He wished us safe sailing, making it clear he couldn't stay. His wife sat in the car at the head of dock, staring straight ahead. We'd been given quite a cellar of bon voyage bottles; we'd been joking about the stowage problem, but I found myself unexpectedly touched by this gesture. In his eyes and in his handshake I could tell we would have a vicarious stowaway.

9

July 20, five days out, a foggy night, drizzle and occasional rain, wind Force 3 (about ten knots) from the southwest, 620 miles to Achill Head. Because we're sailing downwind, there's little apparent wind. The air is soupy; the cabin is dank, close. We move in a smothering cocoon of cottony gray; in the gloom only the nearest whitecaps are visible, brilliantly phosphorescent, dim footlights to our passing. With the wind from behind, we're not stabilized by it as we are when it presses on the sails from abeam: we're rolling. Even though all is well—the breeze moderate, the boat very little stressed, our speed fairly good—to me it is an uneasy way to go along. On other, more upwind points of sail, when *Clarity* heels to the wind, her sails and rig taut, muscles toned, she seems right, ready. This slack shifting—the jib puffy, occasionally collapsing—feels disquietingly passive, vulnerable.

My mind's eye lifts off overhead to a space shuttle position from where, despite night and fog, I can clearly see flotillas of million-ton Ultra-Large Crude Carriers steaming out of the English Channel, then fanning out to slice the ocean all around us. *Clarity* inches blindly along, like a woolly bear caterpillar on the interstate. I can't tell whether radar screens are being consulted, or courses altered. After entertaining this train of thought for a while, I go below and call on the radio: "This is the sailing vessel *Clarity, Clarity, Clarity,* calling any ships in the area to alert you to our presence. Our position is . . . ," then the latitude-longitude coordinates from the Loran. For the rest of the night we make such calls every forty-five minutes, figuring that's how long it would take a ship to get to us from the limit of our radio range.

Between radio calls, I sit in the companionway listening on the Walkman to the Beatles' *Abbey Road,* over and over. At the time the album came out I was not one to notice lyrics. Even now I usually require a cue from a friend before it occurs to me to pay attention to them. There is simply no excuse for this. I've certainly shed my share of tears over lyrics, sure that certain songs were written just for me. It is just laziness. I haven't even gone back to scoop up what I've missed, even from such essentials of the canon as

Abbey Road. Now, when it is in my best interest to distract myself from the realities at hand, I smile at what was there all along. My mental screen surveys the shady garden of an octopus and, true enough, it does seem like years since we've seen the sun.

Listening to the exploits of Maxwell Edison and his silver hammer, I find that, while unaware of ever having taken them in, I can sing along word for word on the second hearing. Warehouses full of such stealthily imprinted matter stock my mind, all minds, entering by osmosis while I sit stupidly at the gate, thinking I know what I'm thinking.

On Brian's watch, the wind comes and goes, leaving us rolling in the leftover waves. The sails slat limply, collapsing, filling, collapsing, filling, with a snap that resounds in the rigging. Down below, it's as though we're in a string bass being carried clumsily down a flight of stairs.

Dawn of the sixth day brings a thinning of the fog, a little sun, then more and more, and a light steady breeze. The opening out of the horizon is a tonic after the closed-in night. Soon we're drying out damp berth cushions on deck. At 1700 hours, the Loran says 599 to Horta, 600 to Achill Head. We break out bubbly white Portuguese wine and Portuguese cheese for a celebration in the sunny cockpit.

At 0445 the next morning, Brian is making a log entry noting a new breeze filling in from the southeast, Force 3–4, when he makes a routine check of the barograph. During the night the needle has traced a dramatic plunge— very bad news, a deep depression coming through. I wake up to this word. My brain sputters out feeble, futile protests: the instrument must be wrong . . . I crave corroboration. We haven't seen a ship in five days. For only $1600 you could have gotten a single-sideband radio that would pick up weather broadcasts anywhere in the world. But no—got to be self-reliant, no more gadgets, you said. So what did you get? A stereo, a cockpit table. So now are you happy?

Though we're reaching pleasantly under a gray sky with unlimited visibility, suddenly we're tense, waiting. Images tumble into my mental hopper of a wall of wind, sharp-edged as a tornado, headed our way. Actually, at the moment we need more sail to keep our speed up.

While we're lowering the small jib, the halyard wraps itself around the radar reflector. Brian and Bob haul me aloft in the bos'un's chair to untangle it. I have a Walter Mittyish feeling that the score should swell to full orchestra. I've been aloft under way before, but never out at sea, and never with a barograph downspike lurking in the cabin. With the broader horizon from thirty-five feet up the mast, I pick out the derricks of a ship I couldn't see from on deck.

They lower me to the deck and we proceed with the sail change. I feel rushed, irritable, as though the ship might vanish, as though we're tempting fate by putting up more sail. Actually the ship is getting closer; we can see it now from the deck. I call on the radio to ask for the High Seas Forecast. A southern accent comes back; the ship is the *Sheldon Lakes* from New Orleans.

He reads us the forecast: Strong Gale, Force 9.

"This is not good news," I reply, my voice stony flat. I am giving him a chance to look hard at the slip of paper and try again, as a defendant imagines challenging the foreman of the jury. But there is hope. The captain is puzzled; his barograph has taken the same plunge as ours but has already started climbing again. We peer at ours and manage to conclude that yes, that last millimeter of ink is, well, at least plunging less steeply. Maybe the low has passed safely to the north of us.

All morning and afternoon we reach at good speed. I am morose, like a patient waiting for test results, running through endless emergency drills in my head, not believing for a minute our announced conclusion that the gale has missed us. Bob has the clear-eyed good cheer of a true believer in chain of command: he's been told all's well; that's the word until he hears otherwise. He's not unaware of my vibes: at one point he looks down into the cabin, where I've taken to my berth for some serious worrying, and says, "This is sailing at its best. I'll tell you something Willy, sitting out here is better than getting laid."

During the day the breeze freshens and we reduce sail in stages until we've taken the third and deepest reef in the mainsail, not unusual when we're sailing downwind and don't need a lot of sail power to maintain good speed. In the evening the wind decreases, enough so that, as it's getting dark, usually a time for sail reduction, we crack out the third reef and head into the night watches with just two, more temptation than fate can resist.

At 0330, Brian calls all hands on deck to put the third reef back in. Bob and I groggily flail in the cabin. The suiting up routine, now that we've reached forty-nine degrees north (the latitude of Newfoundland), has taken on more layers: socks, sweaters, long pants under the foul-weather gear. It seems to take forever, but it is essential to be warm and dressed for staying out all night, in case. Brian's call was studiedly level-voiced, but the sea against the hull sounds like we're rafting on the Colorado River; the halyards drum on the mast, louder in the gusts; I'm properly agitated.

We want all three on deck in these conditions so that one can be a spotter, as in gymnastics. The biggest fear is of a man overboard. Brian is wide awake and accustomed to the conditions, so he goes to the job at the mast, his safety line clipped to the boat as he goes forward. I'm at the halyard winch in the cockpit. Bob watches, ready to assist.

At Brian's OK, I ease the tension on the main halyard, and begin to pay it out, lowering the sail slowly under control, as Brian hauls it down manually at the mast. When he has it down to the third reef point, he attaches the new bottom forward corner of the sail to the reefing hook on the boom and he bellows "OK!" again, now having to be heard over the buffeting of the loose sail. I release the main sheet, letting the boom out so the sail's fullness won't resist as Brian hauls on the line that pulls the new bottom aft corner of the sail in tight to the boom. This is the hardest part. Brian is crouched on deck, the loose lowered portion of the sail billowing around him. He strains on the line, but cannot see the result. I tell him how he's doing, in my loudest voice short of a blood-curdling scream. We don't have cause to shout in our lives, so this hollering, meant to be emotionally neutral, is still disconcerting. Hauling on the line, then securing what he's gained with a turn on the cleat, then hauling again, he finally snugs it in. I re-tension the main halyard, then pull in the sheet. The sail fills, we accelerate, things quiet down. Brian sets about gathering in the loose lower part of the sail and tying it along the boom. I always sense gratitude from *Clarity* when we relieve her stress. She leaps along now, still quickly, but corking over rather than slamming into the waves.

When Brian returns to the cockpit, we sit in a row on the windward side, talking it over like athletes at halftime, seeing how she's doing. It is heady, bringing off a smooth job of reefing in these conditions, my man and I, an able team. Our voices are excited, proud; I feel potent, clear-headed, as though I could stay up for days.

The wind piles in thicker and thicker through the wee hours. It is from the west, we're headed northeast, so it is a fair wind on our port quarter. We're tearing along in waves so big that we experience a slight lull in each trough, a gust on each crest.

Clarity is driven by so much excess power that she is steadily exceeding her hull speed. In normal conditions, a keel hull like *Clarity*'s generates a wave system, nestling between its bow wave and its stern wave as it moves through the water. The greater the distance between the two wave crests, the faster the wave system can move; thus, the bigger the keel boat, the

Gale seas. When we careen off the crest of each wave, our stern wave sums with the crest, heaping up into a pile of water that topples with a roar and a smack on our behind. It's hard to avoid the conclusion that we are not wanted here.

faster—tycoons had to love it. Under the present press of limitless horsepower, *Clarity* is trying to overtake her own wave system, burrowing into her bow wave and outrunning her stern wave, leaving it breaking in our wake in a swath of white froth. When we careen off the crest of each wave, our breaking stern wave sums with the crest, heaping up into a pile of water that topples with a roar and a smack on our behind. *Clarity*'s full, buoyant rear rises quickly each time; we are not taking seas aboard.

If this were a summer Saturday with twelve miles of this to do before safe harbor, we'd be riding on the bow pulpit, whooping like bronco busters; later, at anchor, we'd be bursting with righteous zealotry. Instead, it is a summer Saturday with 389 miles to go to Achill Head, and with the fear that this could get worse. At 0715 we drop the main.

Even with just the tiny forestaysail, we continue to hurtle along. Minute by minute, the brute weight of wind muscles the waves into larger and larger, better defined, great, rumbling combers, their broad, steep slopes scoured with serrations as though from helicopter wash.

Thus reduced to a scrap of sail, still on a sleigh ride, we enter onto the gray area between the tactics of normal sailing and those of survival. I resist the transition, as I resist first putting on gloves in the winter. For several hours we carry on at fine speed. Every so often we're shouldered off course by a wave and the Aries heaves the tiller hard over. The gear is so powerful (though it can be disconnected instantly) we must be sure to keep clear of the tiller's swing. Sitting alone in the cockpit, I study the churning avalanches chasing us, each one roiling up against *Clarity*'s stern, but so far not managing to poop us—to break into the cockpit. That is the fear: the cockpit filled with water, pouring through the companionway into the cabin, *Clarity* struggling from under it. It only takes one. Many a boat has been lost that way, swamped before she could recover. We have the companionway drop boards in place and the sliding hatch closed, blocking the companionway against such green water invasions. Three of the boards are of three-quarter inch oak, one is Lexan, a high-strength plastic, clear so people below can see what's going on. At the level of the cockpit seats, *Clarity* has a large elliptical hole where the tiller passes through the transom. This would drain most of the cockpit in seconds; then her pair of two-inch institutional shower drains would quickly drain the footwell. But let's not test it.

Sealing off the cabin shifts our emotional gears. Brian and Bob seem much farther away when I cannot simply glance down into the domestic scene to see someone reading or peeling an onion. Every so often I see one of them peering out through the salt-streaked plastic drop board, not because they think something has changed up here, but to ease the confinement they feel, or to give me a moment's encouragement.

In the daytime on the way to the Azores we scampered between cockpit and cabin without a thought. Since our turn northward—with the outside temperature dropping as the latitude climbs—an indoor-outdoor division has come into shipboard life. All three of us share an obsession with keeping salt off the cushions and bedding. Once salty, a cushion draws moisture, never feels dry, the stuffing clots to something like cooked rice, mildew takes hold. So on this leg, anyone coming below must stand at the foot of the stairs and peel off anything that's taken spray, before climbing into a berth or sitting for a meal. Thus the change of scene from cabin to cockpit, which helped stave off feelings of trappedness, had already become more cumbersome. Now, with the companionway closed, it's even more so.

This is now quite definitely a Gale, Force 8 (winds 34–40 knots), verging on Strong Gale, Force 9 (41–47 knots). What is useful about Admiral Beaufort's Wind Scale is that, instead of placing the descriptive importance on wind speed, he attempted, back in 1805, to define and label gradations of sea conditions. Thus, with no instruments, a sailor can accurately compare one day to another and adjust tactics accordingly. Since Beaufort's first definitions in 1805, many authors have taken a crack at their own descriptions. Eric Sloane on Force 12, Hurricane: "No canvas can stand." Webster's on Force 12 is equally succinct: "Devastation occurs."

Sitting in the cockpit, I'm impassive. These things happen; *Clarity*'s seen worse. We've got plenty of sea room. We're not being driven close to a rocky shore. I have no business sailing to this part of the world if I can't put up with a gale. Then the other voice: No, no, there's been some mix-up, I ordered the passage without the storms. I'm not from the adventurers, remember? I just wanted transportation.

Each of us in turn samples the conditions in the cockpit. I come below and Brian goes out for a sit. It is relatively quiet below, the shrill howl of the wind muted to a moan. Every few minutes though, *Clarity* vaults off the crest of a wave and slams into the next trough as though she were dropped by a crane onto concrete—the sort of hit that gave rise to "shiver my timbers." It seems impossible just now that any construction can withstand much of this, even though I watched David preparing her for it for two years.

Brian has an instinctive aversion to running downwind in storms, even though running with no sails, while dragging long lines, a sea anchor, old tires, or whatever else to slow down is generally considered the ultimate storm survival tactic. We each have our particular bogeymen and his are being pooped by a breaking wave or, worse, being pitch-poled: tumbled end over end by a breaking wave. Even our present relatively controlled roller coaster ride, which would delight an ocean racing crew, feels to him too much like riding a tractor trailer down Pike's Peak with no brakes.

With the wind still building, Bob takes his turn. Coming back below, he searches our faces for news. He can tell it's getting worse. His voice isn't challenging, but, "So Willy, what's our fallback position here?"

At 1330 Bob writes in the log: "Looking for alternatives to the Force 9 Gale we are in."

During the afternoon, we get a confusing weather report from a ship. Speaking in extremely shaky English, the officer first gives the storm's center at 0800 this morning as forty-nine degrees north latitude and seventeen degrees west longitude, meaning we're smack in the middle of it ("it" being perhaps a thousand miles across). Then, after signing off, he suddenly comes back on to say he's located a report from 1000 hours putting the center at fifty-seven degrees north and eighteen degrees west, a change of five hundred miles in two hours. It's tempting to think that we just aren't understanding him. Not wanting to insult him, we nonetheless need another go at his accent. With Brian prompting me, I rehash the figures with him in different wordings. I read the figures back to him; he confirms them. I experiment with a contradictory assertion; he agrees to that too. There are undercurrents here. Despite the meteorological shorthand and the rubrics of two-way radio—Roger that, over, that's a negative—we are still two men in a strong gale, strangers to each other. I need his information; he is an intelligent, proud man who does not speak my language. The convention is that I should not burden him with my emotions. (Thus the stereotype of the airline pilot's laconic final transmissions, later found on the black box tape in the wreckage.) So strong is this convention that, were I to betray a trace of fear, he might well read it as desperation. And he knows that centuries of tradition, not to mention international admiralty law, require that he come to our aid if we ask.

After getting off the radio, Brian and I each enact a sort of meditation with gestures. Moving one hand in a counterclockwise swirling motion as though polishing a window, we represent the winds spiraling outward around a low pressure center. With the other hand we point to where we might be in the swirl, pondering the wind direction that should exist there. The officer's second report would square with the westerly winds we are experiencing. Besides, it would put the storm farther from us and moving away. So our motions are gestures of prayer.

We decide that our galloping progress, though on a beeline for Achill Head, is having the effect of pursuing this depression, keeping us in it longer. We should stop and let the gale do the moving. Also it's getting on toward evening with no letup in sight. At 1750 on the twenty-third, we heave to.

Every boat behaves a little differently in heaving to. On *Clarity*, we do it with just the triple-reefed main. The idea is to trim the sail so that it makes her try to head off downwind, while lashing the tiller so that it tries to head her up into the wind. Once these two forces are balanced properly, she sits pointing about forty-five degrees short of dead upwind, not moving forward, scalloping slowly sideways, kept from rolling by the wind pressure on the sail. Seas break from ahead of us instead of threatening the cockpit.

It is amazing how *Clarity* settles into this. The motion and commotion drop off abruptly. It is as though, after long running with the stampeding herd, we've now ducked behind a cactus that's parting the flow. Balanced, though, against this sense of respite, is the sense that we've now traversed the gray area: this is the realm of survival tactics. Many people take heaving to very lightly; they do it when they want to stop for lunch, wait for fog to burn off. For me it's always marked the beginning of badness. We're a still point of passive resistance to an utterly indifferent, unimaginably powerful, and utterly routine natural event. We're playing dead in hopes it will leave us alone.

Through the night, the man on watch remains down below, sitting at the chart table, the only place in the cabin that's permitted for sitting in full foul-weather regalia. Every fifteen minutes: slide the hatch open enough to peer around the horizon.

Off watch, I sleep fitfully. I know in my mind, and very nearly in my heart, that *Clarity* is just fine, nowhere near as stressed as on a thumping beat down Buzzard's Bay. But, aside from my superstitious fear of optimism, I'm wary of being lulled into unpreparedness.

The wind strength comes in a slow respiratory pattern: every couple of minutes the press of a gust, a raised pitch of moan. In between gusts, I wait the way you wait to see if your hiccups are gone. No, there's another gust. Slowly though, through the night, hour by hour, there is an unmistakable dulling of the roar. Each of us is aware of it, but by unspoken shared superstition we do not speak of it.

Gradually the portholes shift from black to gray, and then, sun. We open up the companionway, overjoyed. Brian takes a picture of the crisp dawn, announcing: "We'll call this 'The End of the Gale.'" The waves are still huge, but their surfaces are glossy, not scoured; their crests are not hurled. The breeze is merely fresh, these waves are leftovers. As he did when we discovered the Azores, Bob releases a great gush of appreciation for our savvy; we modestly agree. Having come through it, it's almost possible to say, This was why we do this, to prepare yourself well, and then go one-on-one with Nature. There's really too little fortitude required in modern life. Besides, now that we're through it, the odds are with us.

Brian writes in the log: "*The Gale is over.*"

Bob and I sit out in the cockpit all morning while Brian catches up on sleep. Bob's relief takes the form of an outpouring of favorite firehouse yarns, most prefaced with avowals of his undying affection for whomever is about to be the butt of the story. Bob cherishes a good story, presents it as though it were a guaranteed great brandy, lovingly elaborating the details, digressing as needed without fear of losing the thread: a style born of the constant need to kill time.

With childlike delight he discovers I am one of the few people he knows who has not heard the one about the nasty ex-wife of a buddy of his, the ex nobody liked, who was in the bathroom on a ski tour bus when the bus skidded off the road and ended up on its roof. Bob skillfully lays the ground-work, digressing extensively on her villainy so I may savor the punch line all the more. But I am distracted. Something is wrong here. The wind is building again.

10

W e seem to be the only yacht in attendance at this re-enactment celebrating the tricentennial, almost to the day, of the trashing of the Spanish Armada by gales.

I don't usually permit myself to take the weather personally, but by early afternoon, when we're once again being man-handled along under triple-reefed main alone, I'm angry, a useful reaction.

The thumping arrival of this second gale has stripped all three of us of our stalwart first-gale masks. In the first gale, each of us tensed his solar plexus and said, Go ahead punch it. Now, after lulling us off guard, the brawler lets go the sucker punch. Brian is saying melodramatic things, for him, like, "I don't like this." Bob suddenly has circles under his eyes, wants to know always, "What's the plan?"

I, for my part, am not only cross but queasy; not puking, but robbed of humor and spirit. If I am up and about, I feel the warning signs of incapacity, a particularly frightening prospect given the fantasies infesting my mind of us wrestling water jugs into the survival raft. If I stay in my berth, I'm OK. I can't tolerate reading, or at any rate the murder-thriller I'm reading is all wrong. I lie staring at the overhead. I am aware that I am not pulling my weight, either in watch duty or morale propping, but it's all I can do right now. I am intent on remaining here, hibernating—so intent that, despite lively imaginings of the keel working loose, I will not move the five feet to check the water level in the bilge. I can no more will myself to cheer up than a potato bug can uncurl in the palm of your hand. Throughout the passage, we've only been using the two single berths in the main cabin; the double in the forward cabin was never intended as a sea berth. This has put a cramp on friskiness—hardly a problem at the moment, with libido but a pleasant memory. Brian and Bob are very generous about allowing me extra horizontal time; they're probably choosing my passive horizontal grumpiness over my more oppressive vertical version.

Conditions worsen rapidly. Soon we're surfing too fast again. White water hisses around the hull; *Clarity*'s fifteen thousand pounds are jostled sharply,

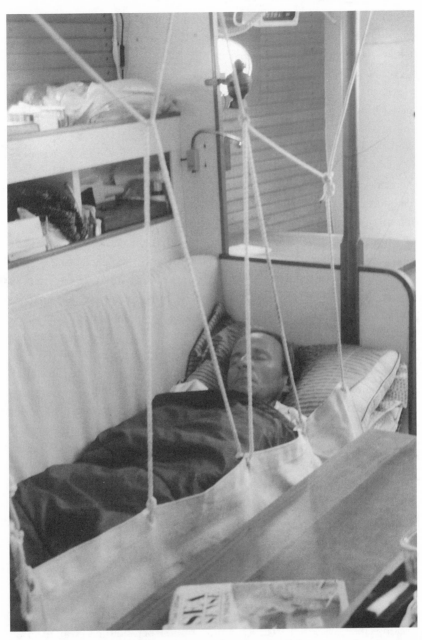

Me during the second, much worse, gale, hogging one of the two good sea berths, with lee cloths to keep me from rolling out. I can no more will myself to cheer up than a potato bug can uncurl in the palm of your hand.

as though we've stumbled onto a bobsled run. This is really happening, there's no channel selector, I'm supposed to be the skipper. I dredge myself out of my berth, suit up, and go out.

Building on yesterday's leftovers, the wind has quickly created huge waves, the largest perhaps twenty-five feet. I do not get used to them. No matter how long I sit looking at them, I still keep thinking, That's the biggest one yet. From atop the crests I see distant, white-toothed, empty horizons; from the troughs, nothing but the nearby, ganging-up slopes. It is hard to avoid the conclusion that we are not wanted here. Our trespass has unleashed this remorseless oceanic security system. Forget that wishful thinking about the odds, forget the cruel hoax of the Pilot Chart, this is simply a vile corner of Earth: off limits. After a sullen vigil, I head back below. Brian and I confer; we do the swirling hands prayer, concluding that, once again, we're chasing the very storm that's clobbering us. We must heave to again.

While we're getting her hove to, my queasiness is in abeyance. I bark a knuckle on a cleat, nothing really, but blood brims from under the skin flap, getting on my sleeve, the halyards, dripping where I'm kneeling, smearing with the rain and spray. I'm privately enraged by this garish reminder that we are too delicate for this. Without thinking, I plunge my hand over the leeward side into the water. It is very cold. We wouldn't last ten minutes.

Afterwards we sit in a row, seeing how she's doing. Bob is true to his pattern—a man used to confronting chaotic, dangerous conditions in an orderly manner. Each time we're fresh from making a tactical decision and executing it, and I am savoring the fleeting feeling of effectiveness, he asks, "So Willy, what's our fallback here?" His presumption—that I am simply working down a memorized list keyed to the Beaufort scale—reminds me of how storm tactics are earnestly argued at yacht club bars the world over by people who have not experienced (and, if they have anything to say about it, will never experience) anything worse than a thunderstorm. They parrot the ad copy for products that offer to reward your purchase with your life. They prove their points with stories they've read, stories that transform solutions devised in howling midnights into textbook formulae, like efficient plumbing tips.

Bob shows signs of a struggle within himself between the clear relief of heaving to and the much deeper-rooted instinct to get this goddamned boat to shore and get off it. It is 290 miles to Achill Head, where we'll make a right for Scotland. But most of Ireland's deeply serrated west coast is south of Achill Head, even closer to us. Bob is steady; he said yes to this total experience; there will be no blubbering or grumbling. But he is also a sensible, pragmatic man. Terra firma is where things like humans belong.

The northern twilight gathers slowly, darkening the hurrying cloud banks and the heaving, mountainous seas to shades of stone. Back below, I again take to my berth for some well-earned cowering.

I reach up and pull *Reed's Nautical Almanac* off the shelf. This is not the first time that extreme conditions have prompted our delving into *Clarity's* library of lightly-skimmed reference books. It was during our first storm, in 1981, that we cracked the virgin spine of one of our meteorology texts to read about the vicious, often unpredicted storms characteristic of the waters we were in at that time.

This time I'm looking for listings of weather broadcasts. My rationale for not getting a radio that could receive shipping forecasts in midocean ran something like this: With our cruising speed of five or six knots, there wouldn't be much point in knowing what sort of huge systems were headed our way, since we couldn't do much to evade them anyway. If we were out of range of coastal weather broadcasts, it follows that we would also be out of danger from nearby rocky coasts; we would just ride it out. If we were close enough to land to be able to consider running for shelter before a storm hit, we would, it follows, also be close enough to receive coastal weather broadcasts on our shortwave radio. These days weatherfax machines—radio receivers that print out weather maps—are more and more common aboard small boats. From the philosophical remove of my living room armchair, these seemed far too far down the gadget trail. Let's see . . . Ah, here it is: Irish Radio broadcasts the BBC Shipping Forecasts every six hours; the next one is at five minutes to midnight.

That's still hours away, but Brian huddles with the radio and the almanac to locate and compare the various carrier frequencies for the station, just his sort of task. Patiently probing among the whoops, roars, drones, and Morse code tittering, he locates a poetry reading followed by a panel discussion, then word of upcoming chamber music events in Dublin. I want to scream into the shortwave receiver so loudly that it will learn to transmit: WE'RE OUT HEEEEERE!

Time bogs down, but not because the hours are becoming rich and deliciously-detailed—rather, they're like boring party guests who won't go away. I glance at the clock: ten after the hour. My eye roams . . . wonder what that author's initials stand for; remember the day we bolted in those chain plates that are anchoring the rig; wonder if they'll hold; the sky in that watercolor is the same color as my socks; there's a hand-pumped, reverse-osmosis water desalinator, cutting-edge technology at five hundred bucks, in the heavy plastic duffel marked ABANDON SHIP; wonder if it'll work; crawl inside a fiber of Douglas fir in a deck beam, study how it's laced to the next fiber; who brought *Don Quixote* aboard? Some spice bottle is rolling back and forth in a locker. Don't look at the clock yet, it hasn't been long enough. Well, how rigged is this game going to get? If you thought of looking at it, then you weren't managing to keep your mind off it anyway, so you might as well look: eleven minutes after the hour.

Is this the same depression, backtracking for another go at us? Is there any reason to suppose that we won't just sit here for weeks, not moving, raked by storms until we starve? Or will we look back and say, "Well, after three days of standing there taking it on the chin, we finally realized that, storm or no storm, we were just going to have to get moving again"?

I reach for the Walkman and *Abbey Road*. There's a macabre coziness to the hideaway where we could rest and be lost, never heading homeward. Maybe the wind is so high it is unhinging me.

It is night now, the hammering and howling worse than ever, and in the dark, more terrifying. At all times one of us stands watch, fully suited up, either scrunched up on the chart table seat among all the wet jackets, pants, boots, harnesses, and life jackets, or standing at the companionway stairs, shifting from foot to foot with a rustle of nylon, looking at nothing through the clear drop board. The two in their berths lie braced against the motion, staring into the darkness, waiting. Each time anyone speaks, a numb trance is broken: butterflies go through me. But we all reply, not to feel so alone.

Every hour or so, without warning, a piece of water the size of a small sedan is hurled at *Clarity*'s side with the force of a cannon blast, sending her slewing sideways down the face of a ravine of water. The instant of impact would sound no different if we were hit by a ship. More than any other details of this night, these rattle us. The slewing down the wave can be dangerous: boats with full-length keels sometimes trip over them and roll over. *Clarity*'s fin keel, with its smaller surface area, was designed, among many other considerations, to help reduce that danger. But that's not what's rattling about these blasts; it's that they come with no warning. They are in the category with rocks coming through the window, knives through the shower curtain.

"Wow. Big one."

"Yeah."

"Hate it."

Approaching midnight, Brian moves through the dark cabin, bracing himself against the motion, to where the shortwave radio is on its shelf over the workbench. Despair cannot touch the part of Brian that does what must be done. Pencil ready, he hunches over the radio with the flashlight. Bob and I lie on our berths, listening. We're like a wartime London family in a blacked-out basement. First we hear a report on the currency exchanges, a dry clear voice, cutting through the waves of static. And now for the shipping forecast, read by Allison So-and-so, and here is a fluty, warbling voice, un-intelligible. We all strain to hear, but only manage to come up with the barometric pressure of the low: 984 millibars, meaning it's bad. This we knew. Brian shuts off the flashlight in disgust; we resume our waiting through the screaming night.

It is only with the first, stingy graying of the ports with dawn that I'm reassured enough—at least it won't be dark when we take to the raft—to doze off. My unconscious has so much static to discharge, the dozing could hardly be called restful. In one dream the Irish public has become aware we are out here; they're holding raffles and drives, sending helicopters to drop nets full of tinned kippers. In another, navy frogmen off an exercising sub climb up the transom for a chat. In another we leave the boat hove to and take the dinghy ashore to go shopping.

"Come on. Up. We're having breakfast now." Brian is making coffee. He's caught me with my eyes open. It is full morning, wind still raging. An occasional zag of sunlight darts across the cabin, but I know better than to take hope from that. While the water heats, Brian hangs up the soggy foul-weather gear in its locker. Bob obediently boosts himself up on one elbow: "So. What's the plan? Breakfast?" I stare at death's-heads I've discovered in the wood grain of the table. The swish of nylon against nylon as Brian tidies is as irritating as someone unwrapping a cough drop at a recital. It's perfectly obvious to me that his effort is futile. We've blocked the locker's outside vent against the storm, the gear will only grow things in that locker. Anyway, we'll just pull it all out again within a few hours.

How does he do it anyway? I've got all I can do looking after my own internal cell of dread. I know he is doing it precisely as a defense against the sort of useless, self-fueling woe I'm mired in. The shred of my mind that still has any fiber knows that I too would feel better if only I could keep myself engaged, if only I could treat this as something to be gotten through rather than something almost certainly final. I manage a few perfunctory exchanges about the wind direction, barometric pressure, and therefore likely movement of the storm system. We do the swirling hands prayer again; Bob is learning it now. With admiration if not appetite I accept breakfast.

That you should not approach an unfamiliar coastline during a storm is one of the few points of heavy weather tactics that the experts agree on. Storm-driven open ocean seas become wall-sided, breaking killers in the shallower water near a land mass, rendering many harbor entrances impassable. By the time you are close enough to find that out, the breaking seas prevent you from heading back offshore. Even to try the most promising looking shelter without detailed charts is suicide. Since we did not intend stopping on the Irish west coast, our only chart of the area shows the whole coast on one sheet. Using it to seek shelter would be roughly like using a map of the eastern U.S. to seek Yankee Stadium.

So why, as the morning trudges along, am I opening the *Reed's Nautical Almanac* over and over, studying the few tiny sketch charts of west coast harbors, reading and rereading the scanty information? It's partly because of Bob. He has stopped asking what our fallback position is, recognizing, I think, that the storm has stopped getting worse. But there's still the gnawing fear that, any minute, *Clarity* could give up. Every hour or so he says, as though he hadn't said it before, "What about heading for a safe harbor?" My jaw muscles clench. His persistence in wanting us somehow to deliver him from this mess is understandable but unanswerable. At first I rebut with the general theory stated above, adding that we're still too far out to make any port before this is over anyway. He seems to accept it, goes away. An hour later, he's back. Not truculent, not mutinous; in fact, once again he sounds like it just occurred to him: "What about heading for a safe harbor?"

But it's not just Bob; I play into it. I undertake to argue against each particular harbor, a debating mistake which concedes that his proposal merits further study. Thus I am tricked into poring over the almanac, daydreaming with unbearable longing of *Clarity*'s rounding the breakwater in the sketch, into calm water. I want so badly for Bob's uninformed wish to be possible, I suddenly understand why politicians make promises they can't keep.

In late morning there are more and more flashes of sun, and the periodic gusts have lost some of their fury. Brian and I emerge from the cabin as though from a fallout shelter. The thin plywood wind vane has snapped off the Aries gear. We have a spare. The sideways slewing of the boat has put a great strain on the small rudder-like appendage that hangs from the Aries into the water. Throughout the storm we've heard it clunking against its stops. A design flaw (rectified in later models) makes it impossible to pull this servo rudder out of the water under conditions like these. We peer over the transom, inspecting for damage. The clunking has chopped through one of the control lines.

Still in the throes of storm-induced lassitude, I groan, picturing the long remaining miles of hand-steering. Brian falls to work threading a new line and devising some sort of chafe guard over it where the old one frayed through. I've picked up a few handy tricks over the years for leading lines through inaccessible routes. No sense moping in silence. I overcome my paralysis, I pitch in. In that moment, the storm is over for me; I'm joining Brian in rallying, in taking back the reins.

The motion is still crazy: Despite our splayed, braced feet and arms locked around anything solid as we hang out over the transom, we're still tossed about; the dainty urging of the line through the sheaves is comically difficult. With delicious patience we try one after another size of split plastic tubing over the line, savoring being engrossed in concrete self-saving. We're sober, all business, but scrupulously cooperative, considerate of each other's ideas, speaking about different plastic tubing options with fervent goodwill. I've seen us this way before, in other situations where declarations of love were just not what the moment allowed. Finally we are successful. We shake hands. My eyes are brimming; we hug. The sun is out. Hell, this is just a gale now. Let's get moving.

11

To get going, we just unlash the tiller, and let the sail out. I steer for the first couple of hours, high on moving. We're running almost dead downwind, 285 miles to Achill Head. It's midafternoon July 25, forty-eight hours since the first gale began.

At 1635 hours we speak to a German-accented officer of the ship *Lady Marina* bound for Liverpool, more put off than impressed to find us here. What we've been caught in is a Force 10 Storm, with a low of 978 millibars, that is now heading rapidly away to the northeast. Having survived it, we're pleased at its rank. Something called an absorbing low is swinging slowly south but is expected to combine with our low and start moving away from us. The officer lists other lows getting organized or already on the march from the west, all tracking to converge with us to the north of Ireland. I press him for guarantees: "Can we make it into the Firth of Clyde before that next one hits?" In exasperation, the officer says, "Why must you go that way? That area is going to be one gale after another. Why don't you just head south of Ireland and go up the Irish Sea?"

"Perhaps we should consider that," I reply levelly.

I switch off the radio; we look at each other. Enough is enough. We're all agreed: We'll change course about twenty degrees for the south of Ireland. Our new intended landfall: Fastnet Rock, Ireland's southwesternmost point, 189 miles. It's ironic to be regarding Fastnet as our haven. In August of 1979, the fleet of more than three hundred yachts in the Fastnet Race from southern England to the rock were slammed by a Force 10 Storm that left dozens of boats sunk and fifteen people dead, making it the worst disaster in yacht-racing history.

Instead of 550 nonstop miles to the Firth of Clyde, we now have just two hundred to go to Baltimore, the first harbor on the Irish mainland, a few miles beyond Fastnet Rock. Harbor-hopping up the Irish Sea will cost us at least a week of precious cruising in Scotland, but having our moment of trans-Atlantic triumph abruptly shoved 350 miles closer is just the trick with mirrors I need. The French sailor-mystic-flagellant Bernard Moitessier was once on a single-handed nonstop race around the world. When it was time to change course for the last five- or six-thousand-mile jaunt up the entire length of the South and North Atlantic, he thought about all those people who would be clamoring to greet him at the finish line, and decided to drop out of the race and continue around the world again just for fun. I'm not like him.

Though all three of us are excited, with visions of long, hot showers dancing in our heads, Brian is feeling a measure of disappointment as well. Before the storm, he had actually begun to picture us rounding the Mull of Kintyre on a Friday morning, making an unauthorized stop at the Isle of Arran to surprise some old friends he knew would be on holiday there, proceeding up the River Clyde on the Saturday. . . . Now not only is all that out the window, but our time in the vast cruising grounds of Scotland, already too short, will be even shorter. To me, on the other hand, anything on this side is gravy.

We continue lolling on, running, along with the gently sloped, giant rollers, all day and night and day. We aren't going very fast, don't have much sail up, instinctively wary after what's gone before.

At midnight as the twenty-seventh begins, the weather broadcast predicts a gale for our area tomorrow. So soon. It is sixty miles to Baltimore. All hands on deck, time to get moving. We raise the full main, held out to starboard, and we pole the small genoa jib out to port: wing-and-wing.

Running downwind in light airs with huge swell is a particular combination of demands that confounds the Aries. With too little apparent wind for its sensing functions, and fluky wind direction because of the troughs, its usual fussy, perfect steering gives way to broad vacillations of heading.

Right after the forecast and sail change I'm on for the graveyard watch and decide once again to take the helm. There is a lot of cloud cover, but occasional windows full of stars move past. Forty-nine miles to Fastnet. Every couple of minutes I click on the flashlight, check the speedometer, calculate how long at this speed. I urge *Clarity* along with the same body English of tensed stomach muscles that made me give up racing. Tonight it's OK; I have a mission.

I see the lights of a ship, and set about figuring out what direction it is traveling. It appears to be milling around in circles, showing now red, now green. There's another. Ah! People are fishing out here tonight. My throat tightens. I love them. I thank them for the ancient routine that has them here tonight. We've finally rejoined the numberless millions of small craft hugging the coasts of the world.

Toward the end of my watch, my peripheral vision picks up a faint flicker of distant light to the east. I turn and peer intently. Could it be? There it is again, not a flash but a quick sweep of pale light across the cloud ceiling at the horizon. I hop below, ask the Loran, How far to Fastnet? Thirty-two miles. What's the compass course? Back out to the cockpit, got to be sure. Hold up the hand bearing compass. There's the light again. Right in the crosshairs. Yes.

"Gentlemen . . . I give you Fastnet Light." I pause after the first word to allow Brian and Bob to wake, then I struggle to continue in a voice as suave as a magician's, when what I'm feeling is pure ecstasy. No way I'm going to bed.

Within a few minutes, the particular cloud cover that was reflecting the light has altered: The sweeps have stopped. No matter. I sit, avid as a new father, gazing at our arrival.

What unfolds is a dawn I shall never forget, grand and lurid enough for the sappiest movie ever made. The assumption that I will go on living, an assumption subdued by dread during the storm, now returns and fills me. As dawn becomes morning, there's a summery warmth on the breeze; rich, early sun overheats the colors; we're sliding along with ranks of rollers; sea-gulls, out from shore for the day, laugh at us. Brian and Bob are up; coffee comes out to me. They join me for breakfast in the cockpit and soon every segment of the horizon to the north and east has been accused of being Ireland. Around 0830, there's no more mistaking it: on our port hand is the exquisitely faint silhouette of Mizen Head, a long finger of the mainland to the north. At 0900 we spy the speck itself: Fastnet Rock, surmounted by a massive Victorian stone lighthouse. They can't take this away from us now. A crescendo in my mind: we did it, we DID it, WE DID IT!

The gale forecast, the race to shelter, become cranky little jokes in our day of bliss. This is the nicest weather we've had since we left the Azores. Shirts off, forgetting to put sunblock on our noses, we lounge past the entrance to Baltimore Harbor. It's another fifty miles along the coast to Cork, with its inner harbor of Crosshaven, the traditional Irish landfall for trans-Atlantic sailors. The Reed's says we have a tidal current with us for the next six hours; there are a couple of harbors to duck into should we need to. We'll carry on. Amid the general grinning, Brian and I exchange special, private smiles, our eyes brimming. In between tasks, we keep orbiting back to each other for another hug. I'm blabbing and exclaiming; Brian is quietly beaming. This will be a part of us, like seeing a child through to graduation.

A rust-weeping old fishing boat crosses our path, nobody out on deck, trailing its gulls like cans tied behind the newlywed's car. In the distance we see a sailboat, beating along the coast toward us, our first since the evening we were sailing out through the Azores. So much for my theory that English Channel–Azores was going to be a busy yacht highway.

The coast is bold and green, dotted with sheep like rice grains. The binoculars are in constant motion. We pass Toe Head, Glandore and Clonakilty Bays. At 1330 we take note: It has been eleven days. By now we are motoring in near calm; damp cushions drying on the decks; foul-weather gear and dish towels on the lifelines. Courtmacsherry Bay, Old Head of Kinsale—the names strike me as wonderfully foreign, in my pride. Kinsale is home port to a boat we first met in Antigua. World sailors we are.

In the late afternoon we are finally approaching the entrance to Cork. I bring out a steaming batch of blueberry muffins with tea. Bob is looking through the binoculars at the houses on the hills around the harbor entrance. I imagine his thoughts: Just look at that—Ireland! As he hands me the binoculars he nods toward shore: "Quality housing."

The tide is ebbing now; we motor up the entrance channel against a stiff current. A small coastal freighter passes, outbound, porpoises playing at its bow. It is dusk and drizzling by the time we make the left into the Carrigaline River and through the town of Crosshaven. A gray-haired couple waves vigorously, questioningly, from shore.

In the last of the light we motor up to the docks of the Royal Cork Yacht Club, a low, episodically-constructed ramble of a building on the river bank—surprisingly modest, considering it's the oldest yacht club in the world. A man pokes his head out the port of a motorsailer tied at the dock and directs us to a vacant spot: "He's gone off to Cowes for the week." We've arrived in a place from which people sail off to Cowes for the week. Before we're finished tying up, he comes to introduce himself, Dr. Ray Fielding. "Don't worry about customs and immigration; in the morning is soon enough. Go have a shower and a pint."

As we're getting organized to go ashore, a man and woman in their sixties knock on the hull to speak to us. They are the couple we saw waving from shore. They've been watching the harbor entrance from their house for the arrival of an American boat, *Poco a Poco*, which has missed its daily ham radio check-in since the storm. There are three adults and an eighteen-month-old baby aboard. We have no word for them; they depart stony-faced.

From Ray Fielding and from the couple we hear more about the storm we were in—that it broke the record for wind in Ireland in July, with gusts of eighty-four knots.

Up in the clubhouse, I'm bursting to tell someone where we've come from. The kids just in from their dinghy races? No. Mrs. Geenty holds the kitchen open; we have celebratory steaks and chips with our pints. In the dining room the girl at the next table who takes our picture is perfectly sweet about it, remembering to pull the drapes behind us so the flash won't reflect. Her friends raise their glasses to us, but this is clearly routine stuff. In the picture we look like we have on red plastic clown noses. One by one we make our calls on the back hall phone. My parents have just installed a phone in their summer camp in the Thousand Islands; mine is the first call they've received. For some reason I tell them only that we had some pretty awful weather—not how bad it really was—perhaps to spare them from worrying about a calamity I still can't quite believe we've escaped.

In the smoky lounge, modeled after the great cabin of a sailing ship, I drink another pint while Brian and Bob call. Near me four old men chew their pipestems, pondering the itinerary of a cruise one is about to take down to Galway Bay, by the sound of the talk maybe the thirtieth such cruise. How can I casually let them know? They leave before I can think of anything understated.

Our planned pub crawl gives way to the lure of slumber aboard a level, stationary object. But, as good as the fresh sheets feel, I can't get to sleep. Though my body is presenting a bill for the past week's stress, my mind and spirit are humming, imprinting, assimilating what we've done.

And, too, as I wait for sleep to come, my mind won't stay off images of a young family somewhere back out there in a life raft, huddled around the baby.

Next morning, from the instant of waking flat and motionless, it began to sink in: We're here.

The Irish customs and immigration bureaucracy has the impression, from their agents in the field, that to do a proper job of checking a small sailboat into the country takes about two hours. Our agent, a genial, vigorous young man, arrived as we were having second coffees, and accepted a mug. Right away he noted with approval some of our book titles—particularly the Ellmann biography of Oscar Wilde—and revealed his true identity as a poet, writing in Irish. He was delighted to hear we were headed for Scotland, and spoke the sounds of Scottish and Irish Gaelic, in lines of poetry and in pub banter, for us to compare.

Interspersed with this, some forms came out; a halfhearted interview was conducted.

"You don't have any liquor or spirits of any kind aboard then, right?"

Taking my cue from his eyebrow, I said, "That's right." At that moment I was rummaging for the right hospitality and had just found it.

"Yes please, and I thank you kindly," he said, without a hitch in his story, as I poured the Irish whiskey in his coffee. We three joined in, to be polite.

He told sadly of the dying of the Irish language. Though the government actively supports the teaching of it in schools, giving grants in the rural districts, it has dwindling relevance to modern life, and seems to some to be a symbol of the insularity that holds back the Irish economy. He enacted the scene in a pub in Donegal when the local men think the stranger at the end of the bar is a language inspector from Dublin, and they break into passionate Irish to protect the grants. This very weekend Michael Jackson was giving a concert at the stadium in Cork. It was the biggest pop event in Ireland in years; it seemed half the country was streaming toward the second biggest city. Irish fans were of the larger world.

By the time we all came up out of the cabin to see him off, it was a windy, sunny day, and *Poco a Poco*, the boat with the baby, was motoring up harbor.

We caught their dock lines, shook their hands, and then the customs inspector went below with them for their interview.

When we came back from showers and some grocery shopping, *Poco a Poco*'s crew was talking to the couple who had approached us asking for word of the boat. We sidled into the conversation. The skipper seemed caught between wanting to dispel speculation about calamity having befallen them—he had simply forgotten the ham radio appointments—and wanting to relate how bad it was out there—he'd taken a wave into an open cockpit locker, causing lots of battery and engine problems. During our brief chat, his wife and the baby were down below on the boat. The other man on the crew had greeted us warmly when we first came up, but now busied himself on deck, conspicuously absent from our conversation.

Crosshaven is a town past its prime: Always a fishing village, it also once had a brief crescendo as a modest seaside resort, and is now a slightly down-at-heels retirement and bedroom community for the nearby city of Cork. Years of a depressed economy and ruinous taxes have caused those Irish with money to buy their holiday homes and boats elsewhere—Minorca, the Isle of Man, anywhere but Ireland. We stopped at the Crosshaven Boatyard to inquire about dockage rates. I asked if the figure included showers. The manager smiled ruefully: "You're welcome to come stand in the chandlery when it's raining."

Late that night we came upon *Poco a Poco*'s crew member in a pub, sitting alone at the bar. We invited him to join us at a table. He'd no sooner sat down than he began to unburden himself of the story of their passage. An experienced sailor himself, who worked as an engineer designing sailboat rigging fittings, he had shipped aboard not knowing the couple well enough. It had soon become evident that he and the owner had diametrically opposed ideas of what to do in any given situation. As crew member, he acceded to the skipper's judgment, but he felt that the skipper's decisions were actually jeopardizing the safety of the wife and baby, not to mention himself. It had been a transoceanic argument, with nowhere to run. We offered him passage to Dublin, whence he could fly to Heathrow and home. He was appreciative, but thought he'd better stay with them and see this through to England as he'd agreed to do. They were gone the next day.

We left Crosshaven after just a couple of days, the urgency of getting on to Scotland overcoming the lure of settling into the pleasant day-to-day routine of the town.

As we came out between the hills from the harbor to the open sea, it was a bright day, with strong winds from the land: We would have a booming reach along the south coast in small seas. We'd barely sailed a mile before we came upon men in a small steel fishing boat waving us away from a long, straight net, perpendicular to the shore, suspended from the surface by net floats painted the color of the sea. We dodged toward shore and skirted the inner end of it, then continued on our way. I noticed two other sailboats also headed east along the south coast, but sailing several miles offshore. Why would they miss the chance to sail in perfect shelter along such a lovely coast?

A few miles farther on, Brian, who was lounging on the foredeck, suddenly leapt up and pointed to another line of floats. I threw the helm hard over, sheeted in the sails, and we sailed well-heeled along the net toward shore for several hundred yards, until I was growing concerned about getting into shallow water. Finally we spotted a stake float marking the end. No one seemed to be tending this net, or was that them about a mile offshore? At any rate, the net was definitely camouflaged.

Before long, we came to another, then another. We posted a lookout on the bow pulpit. Some were many hundreds of yards long. After being forced so close to shore, we started detouring farther and farther offshore, until we fell in with the other two sailboats. By now I was fed up and called the other boats on the radio. One of them responded immediately.

"I'm new to the area," I said, "and I'm wondering if we really need to avoid these nets we keep coming to, or do most sailors just slide right over them. Over."

"No, I repeat no, definitely do not try to sail over them," replied the other boat, a woman's voice.

"Well, what are they?" I said. "Why do they make them so hard to see?"

"Don't want to talk about that now," she came back. "You shouldn't have any more trouble out this far. Where are you headed?"

"Dunmore East."

"So are we. We'll talk to you when we get there. Out."

We had no more trouble, though we kept a close watch for the rest of the day. By the time we got to Dunmore East in the early evening, the other boat, which was smaller, was an hour behind us.

Dunmore East is a cavity in the rock bluffs at the mouth of the River Suir; fifteen miles farther upstream is Waterford, of crystal fame. The cavity at Dunmore East has been made a tiny but secure harbor by a massive stone encircling breakwater. It is mainly a commercial fishing harbor with no room for anchoring, but yachts are welcome to tie up along one stretch of the wall. When we came in there were five or six ranks of sailboats as many as ten deep. Each boat was laced to its neighbor and also with long lines to the wall. We picked a rank and tied on the end, walking lines ashore over the other boats, observing the pertinent etiquette of crossing each deck ahead of the mast.

Just as we finished, our radio contact came in—a small, heavily kitted-out sloop carrying a family of five. We motioned them alongside, and even as they were digging in lockers for fenders and lines, the woman began to explain her cryptic sign-off: "When you called us, we had just sailed over a net, gotten our rudder completely tangled in it, my husband had just that minute managed to saw us free with a butcher knife. All the while we were terrified they would see us. They're salmon poachers. Awful types. They lurk about, miles from their nets so they can't be caught, but they're watching. They come by you in their boats, hiding their faces, staying inside the wheel-house. With things so bad, the unemployment and all, it's big business. They shoot each other, bomb the game inspectors' houses, really frightful."

Late in the evening we climbed the steep stone street from the harbor basin to the village. It is an attractive, self-conscious fishing village, preserved for the holiday trade with its lanes of thatched-roofed cottages now too expensive for fishermen. Heavy metal rock, along with high-fashion teens needing cigarettes, spilled out of a community center dance into the quiet night. The one pub was brightly lit and busy with a mix of local working people and holiday-makers.

As much as I was enjoying soaking up the details, not to mention the pints of Smithwick's, I was seeing all this as a waypoint. I knew I was not being fair to Ireland, but in my own and Brian's restlessness to be on to Scotland, I was withholding my full receptivity, hoarding my reservoir of effusiveness. This was partly Brian's influence. Normally nonpartisan, he let slip hints of the Scottish-Irish rivalry bred in his bones. If I would extol the scenery, he'd nod politely, with a slight smile that said, Just wait.

We left the next evening, timing our departure for the overnight sail to Dublin according to Brian's elaborate calculations, written out in tables smudged with erasure, of the complex and rambunctious currents swirling around the lower right hand corner of Ireland. He got them right, but then drew the one night watch shift when the current was against us, and sat staring in frustration at the same lighthouse for three hours.

We arrived at the marina in Howth—a wealthy suburb of Dublin—in the middle of a parade of costumed boats and costumed, reveling crews holding the annual benefit for the local lifeboat. Search and rescue missions throughout the British Isles are carried out by volunteer crews in lifeboats built and maintained by local donations. Distinctive with their dark blue hulls and orange superstructures, the powerful steel boats are built to a standard design and each is the pride of its town. Pub walls are decorated with pictures of the lifeboat underway; cans on the bar ask for your change; waterfront plaques list its rescues. A Viking damsel with a forward manner and five o'clock shadow directed us to a slip.

Here we threw out the last of the Horta fish plant ice; it lasts a long time when the hull is floating in such cold water. We left *Clarity* for three days for a visit in Dublin with friends—Jane Touhey, her husband Jim, and their newly-adopted son Sam—who had felt snubbed by our original plan of skipping Ireland and were happy enough to have a storm deliver us to them after all. This was the best luck to come out of our change of plans; Brian and Jane had significant history together and the several reunions we'd had over the years had been important times for taking stock.

Jane was from Oregon. Brian had met her there when he was on his first extended stay in the U.S., working a two-month summer job in an Oregon hospital in between years at medical school in Scotland. They had met in the neighborhood student hangout, quickly struck a spark, and after his job finished, had spent a month exploring the west coast from Vancouver to San Diego. Brian had organized that summer in the Northwest out of a vague need to burst the confines of his life in Glasgow, to see whether he could get something to happen to him. Deep beneath this restlessness, beneath his conscious thoughts, were churning the same uncertainties about how life would be led that I'd been deliberating consciously in my own life. (It was at about this same time that I was meeting Judy Zappia and inviting her into my life at the dome.) He knew he was attracted to men—wanted certain ones to be his friend is how he put it—but he didn't yet see himself as gay. He had never been clued in to any of the inconspicuous gay people in his surroundings so that he could learn that there were modes other than Liberace. As we groped along our respective paths, we had in common that neither of us was constituted for a casual response to our carnal urges: "Why not? . . . Might's well give it a try . . . What the hell . . . See what happens . . ." Nor did either of us incline toward another frequent accommodation: a secret gay life sneaking alongside an outwardly straight one. We each had a sense that our initiation into actual gay experience would change everything, that we would see life through a different lens forever after, that the sexual experiences would be just a part of a new identity, that before doing things that could never be undone we had better prepare for enormous unknowable change.

Brian and Jane stayed in touch over that first winter; Jane was starting to daydream of Brian in her future. The next summer they took a two-week holiday in Ireland. Her father had emigrated from Ireland; an affinity for the place still ran in her blood. She shared the cheerful pessimism and handsome facial bones of the Irish. The ancient landscapes, aching for sun, felt like home. She abruptly decided to stay.

They exchanged visits between Dublin and Glasgow during Brian's last school year. For Brian, everything seemed to be sleepwalking toward marriage and settling into a lifelong climb through the National Health Service ranks. Mutinous rumblings began deep: Is this all there is? Jane was beginning to say she wanted to be married to someone. She had met a guy named Willy in Ireland, but Brian could change all that. Brian passed the next year as a junior house officer, the British equivalent of an intern, in the teaching hospitals of Glasgow. It was the year of delicate, painful pulling away from Jane; for all that he cared for her, he found himself urging her toward Willy.

He arranged for his senior house officer stint to be in the south of England, searching for something that had not yet come clear in his mind, but that he knew didn't exist for him in Glasgow. During that time, while in Dublin for a certification examination, he paid a bittersweet visit to Jane and Willy. The love was still there, but the break had been the right thing.

His time in the south of England brought with it a burst of new friends, a reminder of the enlivening jolt of a move. The grass of North America looked greener and greener. For his next year of training he chose Kingston, Ontario.

Jane's marriage to Willy didn't work out in the end, which is a legal as well as emotional calamity in Ireland. Her marriage to Jim, her present husband, was made possible only by the discovery of a chink in the church-state armor: she had been married to Willy only in the eyes of the state, but not those of the church; she could marry Jim in the eyes of the church, unrecognized by the state. Neither marriage was double-barreled legitimate, a matter of zero concern to Jane and Jim; but this second one would confer sufficient respectability to let them get started on Jim's dream of a big family.

Gradually it became clear there were infertility problems. They began an arduous course of therapies, diets, counseling, timing, testing, trying. Jane became, in spite of herself, a nationally-known spokesperson for couples dealing with infertility, a perilous role to play in a country where all sexual matters are at least publicly viewed as slightly leprous. After an emotionally and physically staggering string of corrective surgeries, Jane finally said enough; they decided to adopt. At this point Jane's activism came back to haunt her, nearly disqualifying her as an adoptive parent. But they persisted, and after years on tenterhooks, waiting for this judge or that agency to approve each step, they had finally succeeded only when a caller to their infertility hotline asked them to accept her unborn child. Now as we were visiting, they had just brought home their new infant son Sam.

Not for nothing is Brian a pediatrician. Normally somewhat reserved, he lost himself for hours in daffy exchanges of yaps and grins, bouncing Sam, later cradling him off to sleep. I played, as usual, the curmudgeonly uncle who would just as soon not get mashed carrots on his shirt. Each dinner had an undercurrent of glottal gurgling, as we listened on the baby monitor intercom to Sam's breathing upstairs in his playpen. There was a poignancy to seeing Brian and Jane and Sam together—Jim and I standing a bit aside for a moment in a picture that represented so many miles covered.

At their house we watched the BBC-TV weather. Already in Scotland it had rained at some point every day for seventy-six days and was being called the wettest, coldest summer in fifty years. Meanwhile, back in the States, a record-breaking heat wave and drought were in full parch. So much for my Azores High theory that the earth's climate had taken a benign turn.

For Bob it was the end of the trip. After a couple of days spent phoning airlines, he was out with us roaming the streets of Dublin when he reached the point where wandering into another shop wasn't the thing. It was time to go. We hugged on the street—too abrupt, but we knew we'd have years to look back. He returned to the boat alone and spent a melancholy afternoon hunting down all the tapes, the t-shirts, the books, souvenirs, and rolls of film he'd stashed here and there during the six weeks aboard. Then, as all overseas travelers from Ireland had to do at the time, he took the train to the other side of the Republic, spent the night in a hotel in Limerick, and flew out of Shannon. A cautious man had steadied through an adventure that would stock him with firehouse stories for good.

After three days, despite Jane's pouty teasing, it was time to move on. For our sendoff, Sam came down to the boat and showed us how to put our saucepans on our heads.

This last overnight hop—from Dublin to Scotland—was again calculated: We rode the northward flood up the Irish Sea to the narrowest throat off Belfast, where the current pattern divides, then caught the northward ebb toward the open Atlantic. Scotland doesn't greet you with a kiss and a flower lei. You must earn admission. The night was tedious—ferries lit up like office buildings rushing close by in the fog; lighthouses now visible now not; fishing boats playing searchlights through the cold drizzle. But it cleared before dawn, and silhouetted in the moonlight, we saw the thousand-foot-high haystack profile of Ailsa Craig, the rock at the opening of the Firth of Clyde.

When I first came to Scotland in 1984, I expected, being a continent dweller, to find a cramped little country that you could survey in its entirety from any high hill. Instead it was the very grandeur and vastness of the place that most impressed me. Now again I had this feeling that the scale was off. We sailed toward Ailsa Craig for hours, until, in first sun, I could make out tiny craft—seventy-foot fishing boats—working near its base. We finally crept by its commanding bulk and started along beside the Isle of Arran at breakfast. I passed pancakes and rashers of bacon out to Brian at the helm. The island kept coming and coming. Here was Lamlash Harbor, where, until the storm hit, Brian had hoped to surprise his friends on holiday. Despite having the chart in my hand, I kept misidentifying the next stretch of Arran's shore, trying to call it the mainland beyond. But this was not some two-mile long speck like Monhegan Island. This was eighteen miles long—the size of some Caribbean republics—rising to a central ridge whose high point is a 2,834-foot peak called Goat Fell. For years I'd been looking in the atlas at the rubble off the west coast of Scotland, assuming it was roughly similar to the rubble I'd loved so well in Maine. But this was a Brobdingnagian Maine; we were little men in a six-inch boat.

We toasted with a wee dram of single malt whiskey. Brian was home. After ten years, guest and host, inquisitor and apologist, were swapping roles.

It was not quite, however, a case of foreigner and native swapping roles. Brian *is* resolutely Scottish: In his many years in North America, including nine in the States, he has remained determinedly unassimilated, never tempted down any garden path toward U.S. citizenship, retaining his status as a foreign commentator even as he became embroiled in New Haven political issues. And his Scottishness did come down through strong and suitably ancient lineage. But he lacked the appurtenances—the accent, the town of birth—that make for nativeness. Rather than an inescapable fact of life, his Scottishness has been a badge of honor clasped to his breast. As I'd learned when we were among our British friends in the Caribbean, he was pained by being misconstrued as merely British, or worse yet, as specifically English. My indifferent schoolboy history studies had left me ignorant of the centuries of struggle behind that distinction. It is not a cozy sharing of the island.

The Keil School was another twenty miles up the Clyde. There Brian's actual residence in Scotland began—not with pleasure but with melancholy—when he arrived as a nobbly-kneed eleven-year-old wondering what he'd done to deserve this exile from family, friends, and the soft air of the tropics.

The school was founded by a nineteenth-century Glasgow industrialist whose particular mission was educating the sons of the Highlands and Islands, and those of Scottish families posted to the outer world. Now towns drew by us—clusters, hard by their seawalls, of slate-roofed stone buildings, dour but for the grudging whimsy of their chimney pots—and each town drew from Brian's dustiest memory a schoolmate, unthought of these decades: chubby, red-haired Peter Bodies from Rothesay on the Isle of Bute; Gordon Gourley, known as "Beakie" for his nose, from Millport on Great Cumbrae Island; Alistair from Dunoon, object of an unrequited crush that Brian would not know the meaning of for so many years to come. We would start where Brian started here.

All afternoon we sailed past towns, castles, ruins of castles, the mouths of lochs, a U.S. nuclear submarine base. The scene became more and more densely populated, the river more and more busy with ferries, freighters, fishing and pleasure craft. I demanded the story on each sight; Brian gamely dredged up tidbits, happily apologized for being rusty.

In the early evening we tied *Clarity* up at a marina in Rhu, one hundred yards from the sailing club where, as a Keil School boy, Brian had learned to sail. And just as he had done on those three Sunday afternoons per term that were the quota for family visits, he called Aunt Isabel and Uncle Tommy to come get us.

B ritish sailors cook their meals from lockers full of tins, prefer their beer unchilled, and consider whiskey on the rocks a barbaric American custom, so they do not generally cruise with ice and it is not widely available. My readings had warned me of this; I asked about it soon after we arrived in Scotland. The manager of the marina introduced us to the manageress (as she was called) of the bar at the Royal Northern Yacht Club, which was just next door. As a result, while we visited with Uncle Tommy and Aunt Isabel and walked around Glasgow for two steamy, hot days—as it turned out, the two hottest days of the summer—she harvested the ice machine into the meat locker at odd hours until there were four garbage bags full. Finally, when there were no more stages of the trip between us and our cruise of the west coast of Scotland, we collected our ice and set off.

We began by tacking down the Clyde against wind and incoming tide: slow going, taking spray. Just as we earned our turn off the Clyde for an express reach in a protected estuary, the wind died. Just a touch of bad luck; I'm not complaining. We motored in intermittent late afternoon sun and showers through the Kyles of Bute, a passage inside the Isle of Bute so narrow at some points that two boats could barely meet and pass. Ashore were green, sheep-speckled slopes; ledge outcrops interspersed with pockets of bracken and heather; a few dignified, modest stone houses; and at moorings, a few small yachts of purpose, well looked after—the details of the scene were sober, enduring.

Once through the Kyles and motoring in front of the town of Tigna-bruaich, we met the *Waverley,* a lean, immaculately-maintained side-wheeler, one hundred years old and flagship of the Caledonian-MacBrayne fleet that provides all the ferry service to the Scottish islands. She plies the vicinity of the Clyde, and despite her picture being in every pub and on placemats in every souvenir shop, in the flesh she was still a stirring sight.

We were coming to Tignabruaich for charts. Friends from the Caribbean, Mike and Mitty Beal, had been storing their boat here for five years in the stubborn hope that they might get back some summer for more Scottish cruising, hard to manage around Mike's work as a professional skipper of large, private yachts. Mike had offered us the use of his charts and had given us the name of their friend Bill McDowell, whose closets were stuffed with anything from Mike's boat that might be prone to mildew. Mike hadn't mentioned that Bill was eighty-three.

We'd warned him we were coming, and now we picked up a mooring in front of his house, one of the free moorings put in here and there by the government to stimulate the local pub trade.

Bill greeted us wearing woolen knee breeches, knee socks, a heavy pullover, and tweed sport jacket, his shoes shined, his bearing erect. He apologized for no longer being a drinking man and therefore having no proper whiskey to offer. We assured him the sherry would be fine. He led us to the closet where the charts were stored. Mike had also not told us he had every single chart of the British Isles and quite a few of Scandinavia in these large double-bagged bales. The sight of them set Bill to reminiscing about his own cruising days with his wife. It was quickly evident that he was a man who divided his life into the part before and the part after her death a few years earlier. Tenderly though he spoke of her, the reason he gave for giving up sailing was neither her death nor his age, but the difficulty of finding crew that would put up with his bossing.

Before long he was on to the happier subject of his years in Shanghai with the J & P Coats, Ltd. thread company. He took us through the house; much of his furniture had come from the Far East. Just as Brian's father, in the far-flung Scottish tradition, had "gone out" to Trinidad, and Brian had gone out to America, Bill had gone out to China—a fitting first encounter for Brian's homecoming cruise.

He warmed to his subjects, savoring an audience new to his repertoire. He told of the fall of Shanghai to the Communists in May of 1949. Knowing his car could be provocative in the melee, he had walked through the streets to the sanctuary of his country club. His appreciation of the Chinese waitresses at the club was undimmed by the swirl of those events or the passage of forty years. He added that he had never thought much of the Communists' prospects for running the thread business.

It was getting to be time for high tea, the evening meal. Brian and I made moves to look through the charts and be on our way. Once again he strenuously apologized: "It's terrible me not offering you a meal. As I say, I'm eighty-three, I'm not eating much anymore. I go next door to the hotel for my one meal a day. Wonderful, the girls working there." His gaze grew fond and distant. He came to, winked: "Well, I suppose they may be married."

Then he had an idea. "We could put something together for you if you'll cook it. I'm not too handy in the kitchen." Normally Brian is Britishly firm about refusing such impromptu offers from strangers, but we were already ravenous, and still hadn't sorted through the charts. So, while Brian covered the floor in the lounge (living room) with charts, I made a meal from frozen turkey burgers, fried eggs, baked beans, and toast.

Back aboard, it was the first night that we were neither under way at sea nor tied up in a marina since we had left Connecticut. By morning, sleep had become impossible as we began bouncing around in a strong, unpredicted breeze from the one direction the anchorage was open to. Nothing but a little more bad luck.

A blustery day's sailing brought us to a night of steady rain in the basin at one end of the Crinan Canal. We celebrated the eighth anniversary of *Clarity*'s launching with a meal of Scottish lamb roasted with garlic and rosemary, wild rice with vegetables, raspberries and cream, fresh-baked carrot cake, and champagne. The carrot cake was an excuse to have the oven on a little longer.

Built in 1790, the Crinan Canal lifts you up and over the Mull of Kintyre in six and a half miles and fifteen locks, saving an eighty-mile sail around the Mull through rugged waters. The lock gates and the sluices for filling and emptying the chambers are hand-operated by the users. The locks are too small for modern cargo vessels; the heavy traffic is now entirely pleasure craft and a few fishing boats. Four boats *Clarity*'s size can just fit wall to wall, end to end. Our four-pack included a couple on the maiden voyage of their new boat, home to Inverness; an English family with three kids, one of whom was a recalcitrant teenager; and a tiny motorsailer whose wheelhouse was completely stuffed with its owner, his head and shoulders sticking out of the overhead hatch as he ordered his grandson around during maneuvers.

Motoring along this hillside ditch, we could see, whenever the mist parted, the Sound of Jura ahead and Loch Fyne behind. On the banks were stone cottages among hollyhocks and roses, the householders parting lace curtains to wave. At midcanal in a large stone house was an Indian restaurant, a popular overnight stop. We carried on straight through in six strenuous hours.

Leaving the final lock, we got sail up, hurriedly consulted the tide tables to make sure it was possible to proceed, and set out across the Sound of Jura, through Dorus Mor, a famous tide rip with eight-knot currents that, if we got them wrong, would haul us smartly backward even at full throttle ahead. The currents were relatively favorable for us, but still swept us lustily sideways, in large standing waves like rapids, so that we had to angle our course diagonally upstream to avoid being swept onto the ledges flanking the channel. Safely spit out the other side, we next had to make a determined right turn to avoid being sucked into the Gulf of Corryvreckan, an even more notorious hazard, the roaring of whose whirlpools and tidal overfalls is said to be audible six miles away in Crinan. Though one of our Coastal Pilots pooh-poohed the tales of trawlers being sucked under by the maelstrom at Corryvreckan, the other guide, unfailingly laconic, described a passage through at flood tide with westerly swell running as "unthinkable."

It was in sailing up the Sound of Jura in intermittent rain that I first sensed the haunted emptiness of the western coast and islands. The scoured slopes of Scarba were barely greened by stubborn alpine plants inches high after countless millennia. To starboard I peered through the glasses at a long, bony finger of the mainland, spotting ruins—sometimes no more than a short, brown tumble of wall, stones lugged and winched who knows when by someone making a futile stand. Sometimes, scrutinizing, discovering the fort's perimeter, mind's eye supplying the long-gone parapet, I would sheepishly realize that they were not ruins at all but natural outcrops, shattered over eons. The smoothing over of these bumps, manmade as well as geologic, proceeds so inexorably it is tempting to believe that the puny efforts of humans could never more than briefly mar these surfaces. But the smoothing proceeds to a slow clock; all the manmade bumps appeared in the last tick.

Our British Admiralty chart showed a "conspic. white cottage" which would help us identify the channel between Shuna and Luing Islands. The cartographers were not rash: The cottage had likely been there, and white, for five hundred years.

We had decided on one last marina stop for water and diesel; farther north, shoreside pleasure boat facilities would be all but nonexistent. So we were heading for Craobh (croove) Haven. Formerly Craobh Harbor, a fairly well-protected anchorage, now its encircling chain of ledges had been connected and surmounted by a massive stone seawall, creating an artificial basin completely filled with slips, at an expenditure of effort and money we saw nowhere else in Scottish waters. All this was done in a remote area, no town nearby.

As we approached, we could make out a cluster of traditional plastered-masonry houses, freshly painted, directly on shore from the marina. As we actually entered the basin, we could see that they were freshly constructed as well—a sort of Disney Scottish village, holiday condos. Many of the boats at the slips were English. This was a luxury outpost at the beginning of the Scottish wilderness.

After we tied up and had showers and dinner, we went up to the "Pub." The place was detailed pubbishly at customer level, but, in the dark volumes above the ceiling joists, it lapsed, like a sound stage, into contemporary utility building. We chatted with the barman, a red-haired local boy. He asked where we were headed. Brian replied that we planned to be in Port Appin the next day to reunite with his medical school roommate, Iain McNicol. The boy said, "He beat my father out for G.P. there. Well, it was his father before him, you know. Guess that's why." He said this lightly. He would be quitting as barman and heading back to university in a week or so. Walking back out along the creaking, modular aluminum docks, I reflected that it had never occurred to me that this sort of instant repro village—blandly commercial, staffed by locally grown college material—would exist out here. The present had arrived here after all.

Back aboard, we did our homework for the next day's sailing, hauling out the great bale of charts to make a selection and poring over tide tables and sailing directions. Looking back on Dorus Mor and Corryvreckan and forward to tomorrow's transit of Cuan Sound, I understood why sailors in the British Isles are all obsessed collectors of obscure, out-of-print tidal current diagrams, passed along in mist-soaked photocopies like underground newspapers.

The next day began still, gray, warm. We whooshed through Cuan Sound, impelled by a five-knot current, taking the prescribed bearings ahead and behind on certain crags lining up with certain distant gaps between islands to keep us clear of ledges on either side of a channel barely a hundred feet wide. The hills all about were luminous damp green in the flat light. Then out into the broad expanse of the Firth of Lorne, glassy, nearly empty of boats and thus devoid of scale. We motored along watching a black sky coming up behind from the open sea, dangling sheets of rain. As it drew over the steep Isle of Mull on the port hand, zig-zagging streams—burns—swelled and whitened with tumbling water.

The rain caught up with us and pelted us up Kerrera Sound. It was a day

that, back home, would have made me scowl as I ran ⸻
But I was content, standing at the helm, water drizzling ⸻
my neck. Scotland offers raw beauty in such abundan⸻
think, if you're rationalizing being a good sport, that s⸻
to boot would be like an oversweet dessert.

Oban came by as though in a dream. Why in all th⸻
there suddenly be this dense waterfront of dour Victorian hotels? ⸻
those people—were they driven by desperate loneliness to come in from the
hills for that traffic jam?

We passed from the Sound into Loch Linnhe, got sail up, and reached
in gradual clearing with hot soup the last few miles to Port Appin. A gale
was predicted for the next day, and we had selected a particular cove of Loch
Creran as the best protected, knowing that it would be a long hike to the
village. When we got there nearly the entire cove was taken up with a huge
floating fish farm. We settled for a different cove much closer to Port Appin.
We had just anchored when we noticed a woman riding a bicycle on the
lane across the head of the cove. Getting the binoculars we saw that it was
Winnie McNicol, Iain's wife, and we began shouting and waving. One of
the rarest, finest pleasures of cruising is to sail to a distant cruising ground
full of anticipation and then to have that moment of first spotting the friend
ashore. Within a few minutes we collected our toothbrushes, dirty laundry,
the Yale sweatshirts for the kids, a bag of the coveted American cookies, and
rowed ashore for an emotional reunion.

Port Appin is a scattering of pleasant, mostly old houses, a couple of
shops, a temporarily defunct pub, and The Aird's Inn, with its scattering of
Porsches and Bentleys, reputed to have one of the best restaurants in Scotland. The McNicols live in a house owned by the National Health Service
two doors from the surgery. Their front windows look across the lane and
down a pasture to Loch Linnhe, with islands strewn up the middle and
mountains opposite.

Iain greeted us and before long we were leaning on the kitchen counter,
debating the choice between his homemade beer and a single malt whisky
from his collection. Iain's conversational momentum built steadily from a
reserved, quiet start to a rapid, quiet, mumbling rush. Winnie was lively
from the start. We mentioned where we had tied up the night before. "Oh,
Craobh Haven, that's for the White Settlers," she snorted. "The yuppies
from the south of England." We settled in for a night of catching up.

there were our sea stories. Iain and Winnie were keen sailors, though
ble to do it much anymore, with the manacle of constant beeper cover-
e. They had a small cruising boat at a mooring in front of the village.

Then there was the gossip about classmates and talk about work. One of
the largest granite quarries in the world had started operations on the shore
of Loch Linnhe opposite Port Appin. The previously-uninhabited site fell
within the territory of Iain's practice. When the company had sought government permission to remove one of the mountains, it had promised a
hundred jobs for a hundred years. Just now there were far more jobs than
that. Hundred-thousand-ton ships could already be loaded in a matter of
hours by computerized equipment, and giant materials handling and storage
facilities were under construction. A principal market was Texas, where the
crushed stone was used in road-building. It was cheaper to bring a shipload
across the ocean than to move the stone from Texas quarries two hundred
miles by truck.

The quarry work was dangerous; Iain had already seen a number of crush-
ings and manglings of limbs, and a major accident with several deaths and
airlifts of injured to hospital by helicopter. This was complicated by the NHS
system of ranking hospitals. Some of the injured were too critical for the
longer flight to Glasgow, but the closer Oban hospital had no facilities for
emergency surgery.

Iain was finding the quarry work offbeat and stimulating, but had been
battling for some time with the NHS over its refusal to take into account
this large increase in demands on him. The NHS position was that, since
the workers still nominally resided in their home towns (even though they
lived in dormitories at the quarry during the week), there had been no
change in Iain's patient population.

Another part of his territory was the ten-mile-long Isle of Lismore, running up the middle of Loch Linnhe. The NHS refused him any allowance
for the ancient Volvo he kept there for making his rounds, even though the
ferry from Port Appin took no cars and the one from Oban was an hour's
drive away.

Iain asked how Brian's work was going. Brian spoke about the pressure
to publish, teach, design and write grants for new research, while at the same
time treating more and more kids dying of AIDS. Despite the different
worlds and systems Brian and Iain worked in, both were overworked and
underpaid. I mentioned Brian's outrage at the free magazines sent to doctors

in the U.S. with cover stories like: "So You Thought You Couldn't Afford the Impressionists."

Finally the day, which had begun at the other end of the Crinan Canal, caught up with me. I trudged to the attic to bed, leaving Brian and Iain talking long into the night.

Brian looked at Iain's path with mixed feelings. The rustic, pure Scottish-ness of it did have its allure, especially as he was freshly brimming with pleasure at being here, and Iain's work had little of the heartbreaking insur-mountability of New Haven's plight. But that, after all, is what had drawn Brian to his work, what made it seem like it needed doing. The key difference though, the one that left Brian confirmed on his own path, was that he had chosen a place and a focus. While Iain was lucky to have taken over his father's practice, pursuing any special medical interests was out of the ques-tion. In any case, if Brian felt at all wistful about the path not taken, it was not with a sense that the path might still be open. There was no way he could start climbing the NHS ladder at this stage.

Iain and Winnie have four kids: Jane, Ruaridh (Rury), Padruig (Paddy), and Donald, aged ten, nine, six, and four. The night of our arrival they were perfect, leading me to pay some extravagant compliments to Iain and Win-nie, to Scottish childrearing, and so on. Brian smiled knowingly. By the next morning, they had returned to normal. Paddy and Donald got up first, re-maining in a dream state as they drifted downstairs in the grip of elaborate fantasy play. After a brief interlude of their quiet, chirping voices, Ruaridh thudded downstairs. His ethics and comportment grew out of his passion for shinty, an exotic Scottish mixture of soccer, field hockey, and mud wrestling. Within a couple of minutes, the younger boys were howling in protest: Win-nie's alarm clock. "Ruaridh, stop torturing them!" she ordered from bed. "But they're in my way!" "Ruaridh! If I have to come down there . . ." Another day began. Jane hovered around the borders of situations, keeping her distance from the three aliens (her brothers), soaking up the ways of adults, orchestrating standoffs with Winnie, who glided among the lot of them with endlessly ingenious negotiating style all day.

Winnie was a music student when she and Iain met at university. She still played the piano daily and the violin on occasion, such as in her Scottish country dancing trio of violin, guitar, and accordion. Both Winnie and Iain were well-engaged in village affairs; Iain was one of the organizers of the village co-op, a nonprofit grocery and general store which is encouraged by the government's Highlands and Islands Development Board as a way of offering a wider selection of foods in sparsely-populated areas. Winnie minded the phone when Iain was out on rounds, took her turn running Donald's play group, and ran the daily family bus route to scouts, shinty practice, piano lessons, and all the rest.

David and Joan Ross and their two sons came to visit and we all went to the village agricultural fair. David was the classmate who had railed against the striking miners on our visit in 1984. In between watching Ruaridh playing shinty, Jane doing Scottish country dancing, and dog trials in which the owners were more high-strung than the dogs, David told us about his new job. He had finally climbed the NHS ladder to the rung he had set his sights on; the family was gratefully settling into a community without the prospect of imminent uprooting. The money wasn't great but that was no surprise. What kept the triumph from full glow was the price Joan, a radiologist, had paid. After all these years out of the running, the chances of her finding a job nearby that didn't already have a queue of more senior applicants were nil.

We enjoyed a modest celebrity among the sailors of the village. An aristocratic elderly Swedish gentleman on whose shore we had beached our dinghy sent word that we were invited for drinks. Winnie expressed mock envy at this social coup; we all went along together. His large house up a long hilly driveway commanded a sweeping view back down Loch Linnhe toward the brewing gale. That was his red sloop next to us in the cove. We had a tour of the house, the antiques, chatted about sailing. As we went down the drive, Iain and Winnie added a few more details: He was a Swedish rope tycoon, retired in Scotland because of his British spy work in the war, a harsh old tyrant who had had his son arrested for borrowing the car.

We visited another couple, who had just brought their new thirty-two-foot sloop from the builders in Sweden, across the top of Scotland and home, and could now glance out any time they pleased to see her bobbing at her mooring in front of their house. The husband was a retired engineer and Keil School boy. In each household we were advised of anchorages we mustn't miss and told of each sailor's most distant attainments, as though they wanted to be sure we would not outdo them on their own turf.

Traveling in these circles, I never knew what warning ripple of gossip preceded us. We never encountered so much as a raised eyebrow. But I didn't ascribe it to liberal ease. Rather our gayness seemed so disjunct from this reality it could have been a tattoo in a private place, a sack of diamonds we had sewn into our hems. No one had bothered to work up stands on it; it was on no one's screen, so we could fly in low. I pictured Brian, a schoolboy twenty years earlier, searching for signs of other gay life, seeing only Liberace on the telly.

As we harvested advice on favorite coves, my appetite was whetted by the Gaelic names, full of glottal stops; I began to practice the sounds while shaving: Loch Breachacha, Loch a'Chnuic, Uig, Snizort. It was time to be off again.

cᴓ 14

In Scotland, talk about the weather is not just a resort when conversation fails. Note must be taken of the weather, usually right after the greeting. Skipping the subject is considered unseemly, abrupt. If the weather is awful, no attempt will be made to gloss over the fact. Rather there will be a rueful confirmation that this is the norm, carrying with it a hint that the speakers are in this together. On the other hand, if the weather is fine, there will be no sniveling about enjoying it while it lasts, just the proclamation: "This is God's own country!"

It was not hard to see why this preoccupation exists. During our six weeks there, Scotland sat in the way of six gales from the west like an anvil under hammer blows.

Strange then, that it should have been so difficult to get weather forecasts. I was spoiled by the ease of getting them at home, where the U.S. National Weather Service provides continuous, taped broadcasts updated every four hours from stations across the country, and radio stations repeat weather forecasts endlessly. Scottish radio stations, if they mention it at all, try to dance clear of the subject with a few words: "Rain, heavy at times—some bright bits."

Admittedly, in Scotland part of the problem at first was our main VHF radio, which did not carry the channel used by the Coast Guard for gale warnings. We soon discovered that the channel was carried on our small handheld VHF. So we left the main radio on, tuned to channel sixteen (the international channel for establishing radio contact). Several times a day, on unsteady schedules, we would hear: "Securité, securité, securité, Oban Coast Guard, Oban Coast Guard, Oban Coast Guard. For gale warnings, switch to channel six-seven." At this, I would grab the handheld and run up on deck, where I would perform a small dance to see if there was any position in which its feeble reception would pull in an audible signal. If the dance succeeded, the reward was nearly always bitter: "Gale warnings for sea areas Shannon, Rockall, Hebrides, Malin, Bailey, Faroes." We were Hebrides. Then would follow more detail on our area: "Southwesterly Force 8 Gale, at times Force 9 Severe Gale, expected soon." "Soon" was one step worse than "expected," but not as bad as "imminent." This I learned after a day of heading with anxiety and all possible speed toward our next harbor under threat of "soon," only to arrive and listen to another twelve hours of "imminent" before the thing finally hit. For weeks on end, we would not emerge from the shadow of "expected," "soon," and "imminent." Once, in frustration, I called the Coast Guard after an "imminent" to see whether we might not just nip along to the next harbor. I was a teenager asking for the car keys. The radioman frostily—and properly—declined to advise me.

More regular but equally trying were the BBC shipping forecasts, broadcast at 0033, 0555, 1355, and 1750. The waters around the British Isles are divided into about fifteen sea areas, some of them just mentioned, each covering hundreds of square miles. The BBC forecast gives a general synopsis for the eastern North Atlantic, followed by forecasts for the next twelve hours in each sea area and reports from weather stations, all in five minutes. Terse. So terse that the British magazine *Yachting Monthly* suggests that readers practice listening to them at home during the winter, so as to be on form for the sailing season. Some people tape them for a second crack at the crucial few words. You learn the order of the areas and wait for your area and the ones to the west of you, where the weather comes from. Here it comes: "Hebrides, west, five to six, backing southwest seven later, occasionally gale eight, rain, moderate, becoming poor." The numbers are Beaufort force; "backing" means the wind direction will change counterclockwise; "moderate, becoming poor" refers to visibility. At 0555, I would reach over from my berth, click on the radio, listen in a dream state to the list of gales either approaching or lingering with us, and then roll over and go back to sleep.

After all this, the forecasts weren't particularly accurate. To be fair, it is very hard to say what will happen when a North Atlantic weather system hits the high land masses after a two-thousand-mile romp over the open ocean. On the day we set out from the Isle of Canna for the Outer Hebrides, the TV forecast, reported to me by the postmistress, was for sun and thirty-knot winds out of the northwest, the direction we were headed. The BBC shipping forecast was for clouds, then sun, winds out of the south, Force 6 (25–30 knots). The actual weather? Flat calm and fog.

We had debated whether or not to go to the Outer Hebrides. Including them would turn the Scottish cruise from a loaf to a bit of a dash. I, with knee-jerk inertia, resisted the idea, though I had to admit the name Stornoway pulled me. Brian was not absolutely insisting, but it did seem that, if we skipped them, he would regret it forevermore.

On the morning after our fogbound run from Canna we awoke in North Scalpay, our first Outer Hebridean port, to heavy rain and fresh warnings of a gale expected "soon." It was tempting to remain in harbor, though North Scalpay was a Free Church of Scotland village, no pubs. But we considered the number of days remaining to us, and realized that, gale or no gale, if we were going to go to Stornoway, it had to be today. There were several well-sheltered anchorages along the way, if "soon" should abruptly become "imminent." As we left North Scalpay in stinging rain, a fishing boat approached, heading in, the fisherman motioning us toward him. I cut the throttle, expecting warnings. He wanted to sell us lobsters.

The wind was dead against us. We splatted under power along the coast of the Isle of Harris. Ashore sheep stood as still as hay bales among the ledges, their future Harris tweed coats shedding the steady rain. After a few hours Brian appeared in the companionway with toasts of single malt: We had just passed fifty-eight degrees north latitude, same as the middle of Hudson Bay. Somewhere about then we passed the line where the name of the island changed from the Isle of Harris to the Isle of Lewis.

The brick wall of wind I expected to find blocking our path all day did not materialize. In late afternoon we arrived in Stornoway. Large ships were anchored in the outer harbor; on shore was a factory for fabricating oil-drilling platforms. The harbor pinched in tighter past the shipyard, the ferry piers, tighter still past the fish processing plants and the small mooring area for local yachts. When we made the right turn into the inner harbor and perfect shelter, we came upon the fishing fleet tied six or seven deep on the town quay, leaving barely room to turn around in the remaining deep water. Four or five large, saggy-faced seals patrolled the harbor, regarding our maneuvering as though they were retired fishermen regretting the passing of the days of real seamanship.

There were two sailboats tied along the wall. The inner one was a large, steel French ketch of the mothership variety—broad, heavy, with many eccentric homemade touches. We tied to the outer one, a forty-eight-foot Finnish-built Swan registered in Portland, Oregon, only the second U.S. boat we had seen.

Brian said he had not been to Stornoway in nineteen and a half years, half his life—not since the summer he had learned all the songs of the Beach

Isle of Harris, Outer Hebrides. We took many long, squishing hikes through the heather, on this coldest, wettest summer in seventy-six years.

Boys. On that occasion he had been visiting his Keil schoolmate Sandy Graham, and it was Sandy he now wanted to call.

Heading ashore, we met our American neighbor while climbing across his deck. He was a filmmaker who, since buying his boat in Finland five years before, had cruised for three months each summer, and stored the boat for the winter wherever he found himself come September. He announced that the evening meal, his famous risotto, would be served presently aboard the French boat, since only they had room for twelve at the table, and he invited us to join them. We demurred, expecting to have Sandy aboard *Clarity* for dinner. The chef insisted we at least have a taste, so I agreed to stop aboard while Brian phoned; he would join us when he got back.

Boarding the French boat, I descended a carpeted spiral stair into a large cabin with carpeted walls and large paintings in movie theater lobby cubist style. The chef immediately served me a bowl of risotto. A demonstrative French woman ordered me to make myself at home for the evening, seating me at a small built-in table away from the huge main table. My quick taste of risotto was seizing up in the bowl as the party straggled in from unsuspected nether regions of the boat. I was introduced to several shy teenagers who had no more idea than I did what I was doing there. One was sentenced to my table and sat staring longingly at the main table. I ought to have risen to the challenge and hauled out my twenty-five-years-rusting French for the general amusement, but I kept telling myself I'd be leaving any minute.

Brian appeared on the stairs a few moments later, looking equally lost. A bowl of risotto was pressed on him. My tablemate was glum; the main table hummed.

Brian was saved first when someone shouted down for him. Sandy was on the quay. I looked up the stairway through the hatch and saw a tired-looking man in a well-worn tweed jacket. He was smiling faintly but was as emotionally contained as if he were the taxi driver. He and Brian greeted each other with a handshake; they shouted down to me the name of a pub and left. I had the impression that the nineteen years had been too long.

After a decent interval of chewing lukecold risotto, and after making clear to the hostess my utter desolation at having to leave and to the chef my awe at his creation, I burst out into the refreshing drizzle and went to look for Brian and Sandy.

I found them in a noisy, brightly-lit, fishermen's pub, happily bellowing at each other at point blank range over the racket of the jukebox. It didn't seem the best venue for this delicate catching up, but I sensed that any awkwardness had already passed. Not that they were hearty and back-slapping. What was startling was that they were bellowing about very personal matters, rare enough for two Scots in the most conducive setting. Each understood the importance of the visit. It was clear Brian had just explained who I was. I saw no sign it had caused a hitch, but still I felt extraneous, wished I'd nursed my risotto. Without me there, they might have hunted back through Keil School memories, refreshing them under this new light. The conversation wandered onto less tricky ground, but stumbled over the sudden emptiness of small talk.

Sandy had just returned to the island the year before, after living for years in London. He and his wife, also an island girl, lived with their five-year-old son and baby daughter at his in-laws' house in a small village a few miles from Stornoway. Sandy had just quit his schoolteaching job and had bought a run-down croft house in the village. He and his wife had hopes of restoring it and reestablishing the self-sufficiency of the croft, a parcel of about ten acres which had been rented as pasture for decades. His father-in-law, a big, strong man whom Sandy adored, had just suffered a massive stroke. Sandy's face around the eyes was puffy and creased from days of strain and tears.

Eventually talk recovered from my arrival, and a few pints passed in sea stories and local lore before Sandy had to get home for babysitting duty. We agreed to meet the next day for a tour.

By morning the gale was on, though the inner harbor, curled up at the foot of the town streets, was barely ruffled. Sandy arrived, nodded toward the sky: "There's only ever one forecast here: fair to hellish."

With his son Alistair we drove out onto the moors. They were treeless for mile after mile, the purple of the heather dulling into the gray distance. Sandy was in gear as a fine, steady talker and pulled rank to hold the floor against Alistair, who also had a fair amount to say. I asked how the island came to be called the Isle of Harris in the south, Isle of Lewis in the north. Sandy wasn't able to shed much light on that, but did relate the view, widely-held in Lewis, that the people of Harris were darker—"Moors," some called them—that they had perhaps washed ashore after the wreck of the Spanish Armada. As we continued across the windswept, minimalist landscape, Sandy pointed out estates of thousands of acres of peat bog where million-aires from London paid thousands of pounds to fish the streams and fresh-water lochs. He described the routines of poaching: how he would arise at three A.M., park the car miles from the upland chain of lochs, walk in over-land, dodging the watchers' huts, leaving by dawn with a couple of fat salmon. One time he chucked his fish from the car into a ditch before being pulled over by the sheriff, whom he'd known since childhood. He went back for the fish later. A populist, I figured—distribution of wealth and all that. I commiserated on this Robin Hoodish food gathering. But he argued in favor of this trespassed-elitist system: estate owners had an incentive to maintain the streams, free of snags and dams, and to limit the catch so the population remained robust. The few areas that have been opened to the public are fished out and ruined. He knows some of the watchers and knows that some of the sheriffs they call are poachers when off duty. Subverting the class system on this scale suited him better than some free-for-all with Everyman.

We stopped at the ruin of a broch, a double-walled squat stone tower in which ancient Celtic tribes had holed up while marauders sacked their vil-lages. I pictured them wedged in there in weather like this—damp, waiting, like larvae in an old tree stump. We drove to a sand beach by a small grave-

149

yard on the windward shore. The wind moaned, the sea was white with foam, the scrubby vegetation along the barrier dune barely shivered, just another gale. I didn't get out of the car.

Passing more miles of bog, Sandy pointed out peat-cutting shacks, originally built for families to stay in when they were out from town on the weekend to cut peat blocks for fuel. Not many in town heated with peat any more. Many of these shacks, naked, alone on the sea of moors, were now used as holiday homes, a fact which led Sandy to a wry, rambling discourse on the Free Church of Scotland.

What the Free Church was free of was lightheartedness. Founded in the mid-1800s, it offers a haven from the pernicious slackening of morals, the pleasure-mongering, of the Church of Scotland. Free Church membership has dwindled to a few thousand, but this is a point of pride with the clergy, proving the need for their rigor. The Outer Hebrides are strongholds, there being plenty of the sort here who would vacation in a peat-cutting shack. Drinking was out, along with dancing, card-playing, reading novels on Sunday, outbursts of gaiety. Original sin meant that before you were born you had already had enough fun. The front-page issue of the moment was whether Caledonian-MacBrayne would be permitted to offer Sunday ferry service to the Outer Hebrides. Free Church leaders were calling it the worst threat to island life since World War II.

Sandy warmed to his sociology and talked about the wildness of the Scot, the rival urges in the Scottish character, the prodigious feats of drinking to weigh against the Calvinism. As we drove back through Stornoway on our way out to his village, his story was about the time he had given a drunken friend a lift home. By the time they arrived in the narrow lane, the friend had passed out. The car was parked close against the front of a house and, as Sandy strained to hoist his friend out of the car, the body suddenly came free and the two of them lunged through the parlor window, landing in a shower of glass in front of an elderly couple watching a horror movie on television. The woman screamed. The man stood up and began shouting, "I know you! I know you!" Sandy's friend pulled his coat over his face, "No you don't! No you don't!" The next day they returned to repair the window. Before they began the friend pulled out a bottle of Trawler Rum and asked the old man for some glasses. The old man flew into a rage and chased them off the property.

We drove up the main street of Sandy's village, really just a slightly more populated stretch of country road. Sandy identified the aunt in each front window. "On a Sunday it's OK to drive by," he said. "But I'd think twice about walking by. At least if I drive by they can think I'm going to a different church outside the village. Sundays you are meant to sit in the front room and read the Bible." Once again I thought to commiserate, and said I could see how such village life could make one claustrophobic. "Not at all," he said. "It's why I came back from London. These people would do anything for you, anything."

We parked at his in-laws' house and walked across the road to the croft house they'd just bought. The husk of the hundred-year-old house was fine: the stone walls, the roof, windows, floors. The interior conveyed the shrinking of a failing person's housekeeping, one room after another closed into disuse, to the last stand in the tiny kitchen. Sandy led us on the tour of what it would be when they were done, showed us their bedroom and the view it would have of the sea.

While I could picture the spruced-up croft house being quite nice, the situation in total looked daunting. We stood in the still, meat-locker cold of the kitchen, a weight of dampness and mildew on the air. I looked at Sandy, careworn, Alistair at his side. I thought of the aunts in the windows, the drizzling, moaning gale, the father-in-law gravely ill, the baby, no job. Yet here, leading us around this house, Sandy had shown a spark, an excitement we hadn't seen in him before. In some particularly Scottish way, he was fired up from deep inside by the very weights that I saw as so discouraging. I recalled Brian, tidying up and making breakfast in midstorm at sea.

We went outside. Close by the back of the croft house was the "black house." This had formerly been the residence, perhaps one hundred years earlier. We stepped inside. The black house had low stone walls, no windows, a dirt floor. It was one room, about twenty feet square, that had been shared by the family and the chickens, pigs, sheep, the horse, the cow. There was no chimney. The fire for heating and cooking was kindled in the middle of the floor; the smoke seeped out through the thatched roof, utterly black from countless years of soot, hence the name. I had heard about black houses, but had never seen one. Scots allude to them with some pride, the way an Eskimo living comfortably in suburban Anchorage might refer proudly to igloos in his family's past. It is seeing virtue in a short, direct link between oneself and an elemental existence.

We stopped across the street where Sandy and his family were living. We were taken to the front room and introduced to his wife and baby and mother-in-law. They were polite but the conversation picked up no momentum. We retired to the kitchen for some lunch.

We left Stornoway the next morning. For ten years Brian had seen me on my home turf, had built up an understanding of the subtle distinction between those parts of my nature that had to do with nationality and those that were unique to me. I now felt a growing sense of that distinction in Brian. During our visit, he had observed my interrogation of Sandy. He had fidgeted at wrong assumptions he heard me making, but he had let Sandy answer them. He had often chimed in to confirm whatever had continuity from his Scotland, but mostly he had listened with a certain satisfaction, as he had in our earliest days when I first discovered that all Brits say "aluminium."

cœ 15

The sense of hauntedness that I'd first noticed when we emerged from the Crinan Canal had become a thread running through my impressions of the Western Isles. It came mostly from the countless ruins standing engulfed by heather. At home I find the sight of a stone wall coursing through the woods to be a pleasant reminder of past chapters of the land. But these were ruins of houses, roofs long gone, saddening in their numbers. One day, approaching the intricate anchorage of Acarseid Mhor on the island of Rona, we passed an entire village of ruins. By then Brian had read to me from a history book about the Highland Clearances, and the evil that had emptied this place was palpable to me.

In the late eighteenth century, the Western Highlands and Islands were farmed in small leaseholds with large areas of land used in common, with all the land controlled by clan chieftains. There had been a peaceable transition from feudalism to modern tenant leases and many of the chiefs lived in luxury in London. Around this time the rapidly increasing demand for meat and wool to supply the urban populations in England was raising the pressure for more efficient agricultural methods.

The result, while barely a peep on the world stage, so brutally transformed the Highlands and Islands that the region has never been the same. The chiefs set about creating large, efficient sheep pastures and fields for cultivation by evicting tenant farmers. Those who resisted were starved, burned out, shot, their crops and livestock destroyed. These were the Highland Clearances, part of the bitterly cherished lore handed down to each generation around these parts. By the mid-nineteenth century, large areas were totally depopulated; there had been a major exodus to Canada, the United States, and Australia.

Brian had told me long ago that when he first came to the States, he was struck by the wooden houses, so fragile, so temporary. He was accustomed to the sort of masonry house that, once created, becomes a part of the landscape forever. Over the next centuries, each new occupant accommodates to the house the way we accommodate to the slope of the land. But the ruins dotting the landscape in Western Scotland, of houses, of villages, have never had new occupants. They are the tombstones of a way of life. And as permanent as those stones is the disaffection between the Scots and the English.

The more I heard about this disaffection, the more I could appreciate Brian's regret at not having a Scottish accent. I thought back to Tony Van Hee, our English friend from the Caribbean cruise. He was from Northumberland, up near the border with Scotland. A self-made man put upon by English classism, he had responded to Brian's Scottish flag with a sense of kinship he might not have felt for a fellow Englishman, only to find Brian had what sounded like an upper-class English accent. Now, as I saw Brian so proudly immersed in what was clearly a part of him, I could grasp the frustration of being continually taken for that Other.

With the usual gale in the offing, we motored one day in flat calm from the soft, green mountains of Loch Nevis to the raw, cindery south coast of the Isle of Skye, where the spiked-peaked Black Cuillins rise to heights of over three thousand feet. As we threaded the narrow channel into an anchorage with the appropriately harsh name of Loch Scavaig, dozens of seals in various-colored fur coats lounged close by on the rocks, mildly interested, at once aloof yet poised to vanish, like parking lot attendants. We anchored behind a low island of rock. The anchorage was surrounded by a bowl of steep, dark slopes, thinly yielding to green here and there, cut by white zigzagging burns draining hidden mountain hollows above. Wisps of cloud snagged on the jagged rim of the bowl like volcanic steam, heightening the sense that the place was hours old, that the first fish had not yet stepped ashore.

Our guide books agreed on one thing: despite the encircling protection from waves, this was no place to be in a gale. Fierce downdrafts could funnel down the mountainsides from any direction, giving the boat such a shove that the anchor would be ripped out of the mud. We headed ashore for a walk; a breeze had come up and I was paying attention.

From about one hundred feet above the anchorage, a body of fresh water, Loch Coruisk, spilled over a broad, steep rock face into the sea. We hiked inland along its shore for a while and then, while Brian followed his compulsion to get naked and dive in, I followed mine to scramble as high up the rock face as I could. From a precipice hundreds of feet above the anchorage I could see for twenty miles out across the Small Isles of Rhum and Eigg

Clarity, Loch Scavaig, Isle of Skye. White zigzagging burns drained hidden mountain
hollows above. Wisps of cloud snagged on the jagged rim like volcanic steam,
heightening the sense that the place was hours old, that the first fish
had not yet stepped ashore.

and Muck; *Clarity* was a speck below. I stared and stared, burning into memory this wildest, most remote and awesome place *Clarity* had ever taken me.

Back aboard, we set off for our overnight anchorage, just around the corner at the Isle of Soay.

Soay is about two and a half miles end to end, shaped like a snowman with no head. Where the two masses join, the cleavage from the north almost cuts the island in two, forming a slot of a harbor no more than two hundred feet wide. The entrance is across a stony bar that nearly dries out at low water. We entered at about half tide on the ebb, and with our five-foot draft, we were shortly landlocked, in protective custody for the next six hours. While we were getting settled, a well-scrubbed bright blue fishing boat idled in. A vigorous, red-haired man greeted us. We compared gale warnings. He assured us we couldn't have picked a better place for it, and said if we would feel more secure we were welcome to tie alongside his boat at her mooring. We thanked him but declined the offer for the moment. He said he would hang fenders over the side in case we changed our minds.

The wind blew hard across our pleat in the landscape all night, barely rippling the water.

The gale continued the next day, but at least by afternoon the rain had stopped. We went ashore for a squishing walk to the top of the island through blooming, chest-high heather. Cloud shadows raced across the hills; the island parted a march of gale-blown whitecaps from the west. Below us, the fishing boats and *Clarity* turned lazily to the occasional gusts that found their way into the harbor. We took the footpath across the low center of the island to the settlement on the opposite shore, consisting of six or seven stone cottages fronting on a path along the back of the stony beach. Next to one cottage, amid all the green and gray, stood a red phone box, claiming the island for Britain. Children played in the yard closest, which was stacked with nets, lines, traps, and floats.

We had just started along the beach path, past a tiny, intensively-cultivated vegetable garden staunchly fenced against sheep, when we were accosted by a wiry, bearded old man in woolies and wellies, with a cranky glint in his eye: "You the Yanks off that boat? You want to see what your Mr. Reagan did to me? Bombed the island he did. You don't believe me. Come I'll show you." We followed him to his doorstep, where he picked up a shard of twisted metal. "They say it's part of a plane, but I'd like them to show me any part of a plane like this. It's shrapnel it is." We didn't dispute this, but not because we were convinced. It was clear he was informing us of facts not open to discussion. We smiled guardedly. I commiserated to the extent of recounting how we were buzzed by NATO fighters screaming low up the Sound of Mull. Having established that we were docile, he softened a bit. "Come inside and see how a simple country man lives."

He led us into a room off the workshed with a brass plaque on the door: "Master's Private Study." The small room was paneled with varnished wood, redolent of pipe tobacco; it was furnished with a desk, a cot, a couple of venerable armchairs, and walls of books. Here and there on the walls and floor were mementos: framed documents, bits of machinery, a small cannon. Waiting for precisely the right second of our amazement, he offered me his hand: "Joseph Geddes. People call me Tex." We introduced ourselves; he demurred at the suggestion of a snapshot with his shrapnel. He bade us sit.

First he told us the story of what happened when the government tried to evacuate the island in 1953. "They said we were costing them too much money, they wanted us off. I said, 'Fine, you mean I no longer fall under your laws or taxes.' They shut off the post so I had a friend in London send me an insured, registered letter, and I collected the insurance when they wouldn't deliver it. Ooo, the Secretary of State was a fine, fine man, but I don't think he thought too much of me." Other pranks followed, zestfully recounted, with digressions on education, mainland mores, ferry service, the general subjugation of Scotland by England. Eventually, in his telling, the Empire gave up and reclaimed its orphan.

Then he related an artfully convoluted tale of how he had acquired the crofters' rights to nearly the whole island, meaning that, while he didn't own the land, he had complete control over its use as long as he paid his rent of a few dollars a year. The labyrinthine crofters' laws were devised to regulate the prerogatives of ownership and tenancy in order to prevent a recurrence of the likes of the Highland Clearances. A crofter wanting to protect his croft from takeover by the laird was permitted to convey it only to his descendants. It was under the crofters' laws that Sandy had acquired his croft, through his wife's father's line. If there were no descendants interested, several hundred pages of other possibilities kicked in, and it was these that Tex had mastered.

Having consolidated his crofter's control of Soay, Tex engineered the sale of the island to a wealthy Londoner with no understanding of the arcane laws. "That's his house up at the end of the beach, with the high fence. He can't piss out his front door without trespassing on my land."

Then on to his days as a hunter of ten-ton basking sharks. The stone building we'd seen in the harbor, now all but abandoned, had been where he and his crew processed the shark's liver for oil sold to make oleomargarine during wartime shortages. As though merely to show us the process, he produced a hardback book with pictures of the crew with a huge fish, the boiler at work and so on. I leafed through the book and came upon a picture of a handsome young Tex Geddes, rowing with a three-year-old boy on his lap. The caption: "The Author." I glanced at the cover: "*Hebridean Shark Hunter,* by Joseph Geddes."

"That's my boy Duncan in that picture," he said. "He's got the blue boat in the harbor, did you see it?" Those were Duncan's kids we'd seen playing in the yard back along the beach.

"The hardest thing was getting something stuck into the shark well enough that it couldn't pull free." Here he discoursed on failed designs, the toughness of sharkskin, the vengefulness of sharks, the toughness of shark hunters, finally picking up from the floor a wrought iron projectile, about two feet long, weighing about ten pounds. Pointed at the business end, it widened into a shaft that had embedded in it three hinged, flush-mounted prongs that would open out and lock at the slightest backing out of the projectile from the wound. The back end was connected to the line or cable running to the boat. This device was fired from a small cannon in the bow of the boat, the same cannon now polished and on display.

Here a rain shower drummed on the windows; there would be time for more stories. He told us how he became great friends with Gavin Maxwell, author of *Ring of Bright Water,* whom he met while poaching salmon in the lochs of Skye, and how the two trained Norwegian espionage agents during the war.

Feminism was not a theme, but for all the raffish references to women thrown in with the male derring-do, one woman seemed to have won his respect. Over and over, with well-rehearsed self-deprecation, he alluded to the miracle of his wife's having stayed with him so long.

When his monologue had run for some two hours, there was a knock at the door. It was his wife, a tall, handsome, self-possessed woman. She glanced around at us with a sardonic twinkle: "Had enough, have you?" And to him, an affectionate command: "Time for your tea."

When we got back to where we had pulled the dinghy up on shore, we found in it a large plastic storage crate full of seaweed and huge live crabs, courtesy of Duncan.

Back aboard *Clarity,* the warnings were now for a Force 10 Storm, imminent. What else is new? We put out a second anchor and fell to work on the crabs. Pity about island life, so dull, so starved.

I awoke at 0500 from dreams of being trapped forever in Soay. I got up and looked out; it was calm outside the anchorage. We should go. I went back to bed and lay awake until the 0555 shipping forecast. A low of 978 millibars—very, very low—was stalled near Iceland. I saw gale warnings stretching into my old age. We should go. I went back to bed, back to sleep. At 0900 we got up, hurriedly got our two anchors up, and sneaked over the shingle bar on the ebbing tide with inches to spare. By then the wind was strong again, though not a gale. We labored upwind with the diesel and heavily-reefed main for three hours to the well-sheltered harbor of the Isle of Canna.

This was our second stop at Canna; returning to its green pastures and scattering of proud, small houses, I felt at a new stage of the cruise; we were almost regulars.

The new gale got up again by afternoon. We spent the next two days reading aboard, baking a lot of Irish brown bread to warm the cabin, and rowing ashore for long tramps in the pelting rain. During a sunny stretch we stalked a herd of grazing rabbits with the camera. There were two churches on shore. One stood disused, windows broken, its entryway clearly a refuge of sheep, its bland Victorian style out of place in the middle of an island pasture, looking more like it belonged in a sooty factory town. The other church, on the opposite shore, was exactly right: small, stout against winter gales—even the roof was mortared stone—well-proportioned, plain, utterly reverent. We turned the ancient key and entered. The dim, stone nave was furnished with a dozen or so backless wooden benches, painted brown. At the front, a wooden table held a glass jug full of fresh wildflowers.

The island was donated to the National Trust for Scotland by the owner, Gaelic scholar Sir John Lorne Campbell, who has lived for many years in the manor house behind the tall hedge of fuchsia. The people of the island, mostly crofters, carry on small-scale, low-tech farming, a museum piece of harmony with the land, the same austere, insular life that had been led in those ruined villages we had been seeing.

After being gale-bound in Canna for three days, we awoke to a weather report promising merely Force 7 (*Near* Gale) and with "bright bits." At 0700 we weighed anchor and departed, headed for the Point of Ardnamurchan, the entrance to the Sound of Mull. It was a grand sail, past Rhum and Eigg and Muck, reaching at speed in large seas chased over by cloud shadows and squalls. The mood on board was mixed. For my part, I was jubilant at the bright, strong day, at shaking off gale-bound harbor fever. I felt willing to forgive the relentlessly awful weather if, here at the end, we could just have three or four beautiful days to boom on to Dublin, where we planned to leave *Clarity* for the winter. It was not so much to ask; we'd been patient. Brian, on the other hand, was not feeling very well: bit of a cold, a little queasy. And he was facing the end of the whole adventure very soon.

The Point of Ardnamurchan is a blunt, bald peninsula that sticks out like a carpenter's thumb into the hammering of the one bit of the Atlantic around there that's not tamed by the Outer Hebrides. The Pilots recommend that small yachts stay well off Ardnamurchan to avoid the chaotic muddle of incoming and reflected seas. Its crags looked as though they had been blasted by violent forces, as though the entire promontory were a meteorite. Ardnamurchan marks the dividing line in west coast sailing grounds between the rugged and the very rugged. As we had passed it outbound two weeks earlier, the Pilots had worked me up to a full appreciation of the momen-

Brian and I, motoring in evening sunlight with a low scrim of fog all around, having dinner.

tousness of the occasion, both the arrival into sacred wildness and a touch of Abandon hope all ye who enter here. That drama had been somewhat muted by the conditions—we motored past it in calm and sun—but it was with relief now, four gales later, that I sailed past it the other way, into the sheltering narrows of the Sound of Mull. From Canna, there had really been no destination we could sail to during a gale. At least in here we could carry on regardless.

We made a left at Ardnamurchan and ran in gentling wind and increasing sun down the entrance to the Sound of Mull toward Tobermory, picking up a blue government mooring there in the late afternoon. Our rations of decent weather had been so slim it was tempting to keep on going while it lasted. But no, we musn't think that way; we had bypassed Tobermory on the way out.

I threw some empty water jugs in the dinghy and headed ashore to fill them. On my way back, I was rowing past a fishing boat with its radio on when the Coast Guard inshore forecast crackled out: Gale warnings. And not only that: this was the first time on this cruise that we were wanting to sail east; for the first time a gale would blow from the east. Murphy lives.

The fisherman and I shook our heads. I told Brian the news. We decided that, gale or no, if we were going to make Dublin, we had to keep moving the next day.

In the evening we went ashore for showers in one of the small, brightly-painted waterfront hotels that are Tobermory's trademark. Afterward we strolled up the steep streets, admiring the tiny flower beds at each house and the views out across the Sound and mountains. People were hanging around outside, kids playing, gnats gyrating in the late sun—the closest thing to a summer evening I had seen in weeks. We both made brave attempts to Be Here Now, commenting on the sights. But we could have been to Loch Aline by now, at the other end of the Sound. In the pub, it was fortunate there were punks and such to look at, because there wasn't much to say. Brian's knee jigged up and down steadily.

In the morning, we turned on the radio as we were getting ready to go: "Severe easterly Gale, Force 9, imminent." Our barograph was lower than ever. We would be heading dead upwind in a waterway about two miles wide. We stayed.

Most of the day was sultry flat calm. In Tobermory the wind peaked at 0900 at fifteen knots. Was it better, I brooded, to be pinned in harbor by moaning gales, heeling at anchor, or to be pinned in harbor in flat calm by predictions of even worse gales? We made grumpy resolves that on future cruises in Scotland we would go where we wanted, when we wanted.

The next morning we departed in pouring rain with a fresh breeze, again from the east, right on the nose. The seas were mercifully small, but still, this was cruel. I could keep my spirits up all right, for Brian's sake, but I was thinking—and I later found out he was thinking—this has been tiring, keeping spirits up in this muck for a month. This is the last leg, I'm ready to be done with it, lay her up, and look forward to warm sailing next season.

The predicted southwesterly Force 4–5 finally arrived in the afternoon and begrudged us a reach in torrential rain for the last six miles to Dunstaffnage. We picked up a mooring and shortly Iain came with the car and picked us up. Looking back on the day from the comfort of one of Iain's collection of whiskies, I realized that there had been a moment, leaving Tobermory that morning, when, with a rueful chuckle at the pure beastliness of the weather and the finely-calibrated perversity of the wind directions, I had let go of making it to Dublin. In the next two days, as we sat out another gale and Brian's remaining time plainly grew too short, he gloomily let go of Dublin. Time to phone the area boatyards.

All three boatyards down the coast nearby were fully booked for winter storage, with waiting lists. There was one other, on Kerrera, the island that shelters the harbor of Oban. They had room. When the gale had blown itself out, we went back to *Clarity* for the last run the few miles to Kerrera. In a final slap, the weather was perfect: summery, tickling zephyrs, blue sky. We raised the main, but only to dry it out for winter storage.

Oban Yacht Services was in a cove at the north end of Kerrera. It felt strangely deserted as we approached. Four or five large buildings surrounded a broad concrete ramp leading into the water next to a stone pier. A few boats were moored in the cove. They looked like the boats you see in forgotten corners of Caribbean ports: boats with stories to tell, showing signs— gear littering the gull-bombed decks—of having been abandoned abruptly, as their owners gave up on a dream, or were taken away in a paddy wagon.

We reconnoitered the available moorings, some nearly submerged from the weight of weed growing on them, and began tying up to one. A voice called from shore: "Not that one. Go over behind the blue boat." Peering intently, I spied a face in the window of one of the buildings. Behind the blue boat, we found a submerged mooring float and hauled in the heavy mooring line, thick with its ecosystem.

We went ashore in the dinghy, tying up next to a heavy work boat named *Dirk*. An ell at the end of the pier was constructed of riveted steel girders rusted away to fractions of original. It was low tide; we climbed a barnacle-studded, mossy stairway inside the girderwork. Affixed to the top girder was an old-fashioned baked enamel steel sign: "This area is dangerous. Trespassers if not drowned will be prosecuted." Dodging sheep dung, we walked in along the stone pier. There was no one about. The large, hangar-like building closest to the water had a few boats stored in the far corner, each eccentric in some way.

We knocked at the door marked ENQUIRIES. No answer. We went in and found ourselves in a white-washed hallway leading to several rooms full of shelves haphazardly sprinkled with marine gear. There was a closed door at the end of the hall. I knocked and then we poked our heads in. The room was neat, bright with fluorescent light. Seated at a computer terminal was a large man with mutton chop sideburns, wearing a tired skipper's cap. He looked up with moderate interest. We introduced ourselves. He said, "Douglas Craig."

I said, "Was it you I spoke to about storing my boat?"

"Yes."

A silence. "Well, here we are," I said. Silence. These were not hostile silences, but still unnerving. Weren't there things to settle? I mean, I'm leaving my beloved boat in a foreign country. Where is everybody? Why did you have room for me? Am I the only one who doesn't know this place is an elaborate practical joke? I had pictured more a kindly old salt, arm around my shoulder, saying, "I know how hard this must be, but don't you worry about a thing, laddy, we'll take extra good care of her." Douglas waited. "Uh, we'll be out on board working," I said. "You said we could ride back over to Oban with you?"

"Yes."

"So what time should we be back here for that?"

"Five."

"O . . . K . . . , then I guess we'll see you about five."

"Right."

Were we walking with our eyes open into a boat theft ring?

Back aboard, I considered what to do first. I puttered edgily, Brian set about packing. Within a few minutes I let myself realize: conditions are perfect—sunny, no wind, no waves, we're both here, we've got time—we have no choice but to take the mast down right now, by five o'clock. I was immediately launched into action, stuffing my pockets with needle-nosed pliers, screwdrivers, tape, and markers.

This was all happening too fast. Not that lowering the rig was that big a deal. We had done it anchored among herons and bullfrogs in the narrows of Lake Champlain, done it tied to an interstate highway bridge abutment in the Hudson River in Albany. It was not the rig coming down that was happening too fast, it was Brian packing, the end of the four thousand miles together, of the twenty years of dreams. We didn't talk much.

∽ Afterword

The day after we lowered the mast I drove Brian to the train to begin his journey home. He planned a couple of days of visits to other friends not on our sailing route before his flight to the States. Then, a circle would be closed, cross-pollination complete: he, the Scot, would return to America, I would remain in Scotland a few weeks to lay up *Clarity*. Each of us had shown the other his place. Saying goodbye to him, I was struck by the heft of my gloom, the sinuses tight, chest heavy. Why so, when, after all, I'd soon be home in his arms? It was that we had now pushed on past what had been the defining milestone in our future since the day we met. When I returned home, we would be in a new era, in need of a new heading.

I bulled through the blues by keeping busy, starting with emptying the boat of anything that would moulder in the winter damp and stowing it in the McNicols' attic. Each day their close friend Ian Wallace would drive me to Oban, where he managed the ship chandlery. I'd take the boatyard's outboard skiff out to Kerrera for the day, returning at five with another carload of stuff for the attic in Port Appin. Ian's militarily brisk good humor left me no room for moping: the chandlery was booming—people buy oilies and wellies when it rains—and he would own the business in another year.

In the evening of the day Brian left, Winnie had a rehearsal of her three-piece Scottish country dancing orchestra. Perhaps I was just grasping at any distraction from being suddenly single, but it pried open my mind in some small ways I might have fought off if I were at home. She played the fiddle, Peter McLeod played accordion, and Jimmy Irvine, the village policeman, played guitar and sang. Jimmy was a big man, a hearty, clever talker who worked at being village comedian. Every exchange he produced a quip, with booming laugh thrown in. Normally I dig in my heels and become sourer by the minute around this sort, but his energy was so high and he homed in on my reserve so quickly and aggressively as the butt of his jokes—"Winnie, I think Bill here is dumbstruck by my singing voice. Is he not a bit quiet?"—that for me laughing along became the path of least resistance. Peter McLeod was a fit, white-haired man with alert, mischievous blue eyes.

He ran the Royal Bank of Scotland branch in Oban, was past commodore of the Royal Highlands Yacht Club, and was in demand as a toastmaster for local banquets. Despite all that, he had the genuine modesty of someone who is too interested in what's up next to slow things down with preening. His accomplishments didn't rate mention unless they could be worked into a good story. Normally I am a staunch opponent of the accordion, but one of his stories—of playing "The Dark Island" on his "squeezebox" at sunset in a remote anchorage in Turkey and drawing another Scotsman rowing in a dinghy from the anchorage around the point in the next bay—raised the instrument out of Lawrence Welkian depths in my esteem.

I'm not going to sit here and say that, after a lifelong aversion to "country" music the world over, I experienced some kind of conversion that night. While occasions of people sitting around a house playing music have been frequent and important for me, they've generally had one of two focuses: either chamber music in which I, the impostor, was standing in for the violin or flute on vibraphone; or fusion jazz-funk jams based on Chick Corea tunes, Monk tunes, on the digits of our phone numbers, on pure impulse. This is not to offer aesthetic prescriptions for anybody else; musicians just have strong leanings. Anyway it has been years since I played in one of those evenings. And this was no improvisational seance, but plainly just a rehearsal: Winnie calling out in midtune "Is this where we go back to the beginning?" Jimmy sticking in salacious alternate lyrics here and there to make sure I was listening. But I actually started, especially on the ballads, to give in to it. When they did a ballad, all Jimmie's clowning, Winnie's gonging herself for missing notes, and Peter's urbanity, were suspended; the three came under the spell of their ancient, religious love of Scotland.

They were rehearsing for a ceilidh two nights hence, a distinctly Scottish social event. Iain could not arrange beeper coverage and was not going to be able to go. Gradually the idea took hold that I would go, wearing Iain's kilt.

I began by dismissing this as putting on a costume, something I enjoy about as much as a cat does. But Winnie was adamant: I would look smashing in it; all the men would be wearing them. All right, as long as you guarantee I won't be made to dance and make a fool of myself. It's a deal.

The kilt was heavy—several pounds of wool. Winnie pressed the pleats and patiently adjusted and readjusted the buckles so it would drape just so: "These are designed so you can keep wearing the same one even once you've put on a giant tum." The short, cutaway jacket was bluish-green wool, soft as talcum powder. Jane and Winnie dug through drawers and trunks for the tasseled garters, the beige wool knee socks, the sporran—the small tasseled sack of hide that hangs in front, keeping safe whatever a Highland gentleman wants kept safe. Drag has never been my thing. Playing along gender borders was unthinkable in my closeted days, about as far from my disguise as you could get, and even now the concept retains the power to give me jitters. But the richness and fadlessness of these garments soothed whatever tremors I may have had about going out in a skirt. I felt like royalty.

The ceilidh was to be hosted by a Royal Shakespeare Company actor called Campbell Godley (whether there was more to his name I never knew), the present laird of Barcaldine Castle. Many such small castles are under the control of the National Trust for Scotland. If you are a bona fide descendant of the original laird and can prove you can manage the upkeep, you may apply to become tenant for life. With this right go obligations to share the castle, to keep it part of the life of its town. The mainly conservative local people referred to Campbell Godley as "a bit fancy," with a knowing arch of an eyebrow, but no one denied that he had more than lived up to his responsibilities as laird, hosting all sorts of benefits, harvest fairs, recitals, banquets, and such. He had also worked diligently to restore the castle, inside and out, faithful to the hunter-warrior's-grand-redoubt feel of the original.

I was reassured to see other kilts—some, true enough, wrapped around impressive bellies. Winnie snapped me posing in front of the castle, and then we headed up into the Great Room on the second floor. As we climbed the stairs spiraling inside the dank stone turret, my imagination made the period leap. The Great Room was paneled in smoke-darkened oak, with a heavy timbered ceiling, the walls hung with wicked lances and portraits of the forbears who had wielded them. Tables were set for dinner for eighty.

Campbell Godley greeted us warmly, dressed in cream linen slacks, a white shirt and silk vest, deliciously incongruous amid the bludgeons. Our eyes met for the split second it takes to confirm our own. So much for my theories about the provinces; I wished Brian were at my side to exchange a wink but also to note the changing times. Jimmy Irvine took me down a few pegs from the moment he spotted me: "You should have left those legs in pants . . . I see you didn't have anything to hide . . . Why you're probably even wearing underwear," and so on.

We seated ourselves and then I turned to introduce myself to the couple to my left. I offered my name and mentioned that I had sailed from Connecticut in the States and was enjoying cruising in Scotland. "Oh, we're from

Connecticut, too. Essex!" the woman exclaimed, naming a town fifteen miles from my home. We shortly discovered that she had also gone to Juilliard, as a voice student. At first I feared that I had stumbled into a cutesy tourist evening, but they were the only other Americans in the place. Despite my get-up we had gravitated to the foreigners' corner. During dinner there were references to Beekman Place and white Rolls-Royce convertibles; I got the drift that these were not just average plutocrats.

After dinner, Campbell Godley welcomed us and pitched the evening's cause: a new town meeting hall for Appin—the old one had been condemned. Then began the entertainments. An actorish Englishman got up and sang a couple of songs of Robert Burns, closing his eyes in what looked like transport but turned out to be an unsuccessful attempt to remember the words. I experienced a musician's sympathetic butterflies for him and thought the evening off to a shaky start. But the audience seemed unconcerned and applauded vigorously. Campbell Godley followed this with the first of several humorous monologues in which he enacted scenes involving large casts of men and women from audibly distinct parts of the British Isles. Then Winnie's trio played for dancing for a while. I sat along the wall, safe. Next a woman in her sixties, who worked at the Oban Creamery but was in much demand for her Gaelic singing, was announced. She stood with erect but humble bearing, feet planted, and sang unaccompanied in a voice free of ego. All around me, private subvoices quavering with emotion created an eery thrumming underneath her clear voice. The applause was full of cheers. She sang several songs and requests were hooted out after each, but finally Campbell Godley stepped in to say she'd be back later.

Then, more dancing, this time to a piper. Winnie made a beeline for me. "But you promised!" I protested. Dismissing this, she yanked me out on the floor and began flinging me at dozens of other people who were obviously in on it. But they seemed to be enjoying the whirling and stomping itself so much that after a while I had to admit that my bewildered staggering about was not the reason for their smiles.

Then, after the piper cooled us off with a slow, melancholy number, the woman who'd been at my elbow at dinner stood up for her turn and was introduced as an old friend of Campbell Godley's. She started with a sentimental recollection of the time she brought her first husband to meet the Scottish relatives. When she and her groom had arrived at the gate they were piped up the long driveway by the same tune we had just heard. As an American I was embarrassed by her heavy jewels, which stuck out in this unpretentious company. Though her renditions of Gaelic songs were heartfelt if a bit operatic, I was put off by the way she spoke of "our" Scotland, the way old money talks about "our" Maine. Asking around later, I found out that the long driveway led to the Dornoch Firth estate of her grandfather, Andrew Carnegie.

The evening progressed with this mix of dancing and entertainment. A great block of a man looking unused to wearing a tie belted out a couple of songs in Scots English, in a thunderous voice ranging from baritone to falsetto, staring off as though in a trance. Scottish men may often appear impassive in everyday life, yet the traditional Western Highlands songs are filled with tears, bursting hearts, and anguished yearnings for people and places in Scotland, and renditions like these were to me almost incongruously passionate. The Oban Creamery woman came back for encores. A publican visiting from Dorset hollered out some of his local drinking songs. A heavy, older woman with orange hair wearing an outrageous filmy white jersey with a gold leopard on it delivered two risqué stories in doggerel. Campbell Godley's next monologue was upstaged when one of his border terriers jumped snarling into the lap of one of the guests to attack his fox-head sporran.

Campbell Godley hauled me to my feet to do an American turn with my neighbor and her husband. She was willing but the man and I looked at each other and realized we did not both know all the words to any song that said America the way these songs had said Scotland. "I've Been Working on the Railroad" just wouldn't cut it and I couldn't bring myself to attempt "Yankee Doodle Dandy" as was being urged from the audience. I delivered a couple of lame witticisms and fled for my chair.

A woman who looked the picture of the White Settler from the south of England stood up and sang "Born Free," milking it as though she were in a Las Vegas lounge. I looked at Winnie and we exchanged a shudder. This was the wave of the future. This ceilidh, so fragile—rural folk giving themselves a good time (and so what if you forgot the words)—was passing into history. Tonight these genuine, open-hearted people were cherishing their doomed heritage, defending it against the onslaught of Everyculture.

At that very hour, Brian was sitting in a bar at Logan Airport in Boston, waiting for his last connection home, absently watching on TV the baffling American rite of baseball.

A few days later, *Clarity* was hauled out of the water on a trolley bolted together from I-beams and old truck axles. Douglas Craig, a bit glum at being called away from his chair, worked with the yard's other employee, Mitch, a testy Yorkshireman. They winched her up the concrete ramp to where she would spend the winter and braced her with shores of timber. When Douglas had gone back inside, Mitch told me with some zest his side of their five-year feud.

After a couple of more days of next to last things—winterizing the diesel and the plumbing—it was time for the last thing. I crawled into the pinch of *Clarity*'s bow and opened the chain locker. With purple-faced effort I heaved from the locker a plastic duffel containing the winter cover, wedged there in the suffocating heat of a June afternoon. Now for two or three hours I worked the stiff canvas into place, heaved on this corner, then down the ladder, up at the far end, heave, wind's got it, quick leaping, grasping, like an ant tugging at a potato chip. Finally the cover was on straight, cinched taut against buffeting. I crawled out through the opening at the stern with the last bag of stuff, down the ladder, took the ladder away.

On the boat ride back to town, I looked back at the blank canvas shape, my thoughts full of past and future, the way a parent looks back at a sleeping child before turning out the light.

LIVING OUT
Gay and Lesbian Autobiographies

Joan Larkin and David Bergman
General Editors

The Other Mother: A Lesbian's Fight for Her Daughter
Nancy Abrams

An Underground Life: Memoirs of a Gay Jew in Nazi Berlin
Gad Beck

A Lesbian in God's Country: A Memoir of Life in Small-Town America
Louise A. Blum

Development and *Two Selves*
Bryher

The Hurry-Up Song: A Memoir of Losing My Brother
Clifford Chase

In My Father's Arms: A True Story of Incest
Walter A. de Milly III

Midlife Queer: Autobiography of a Decade, 1971–1981
Martin Duberman

Widescreen Dreams: Growing Up Gay at the Movies
Patrick E. Horrigan

Eminent Maricones: Arenas, Lorca, Puig, and Me
Jaime Manrique

Taboo
Boyer Rickel

Secret Places: My Life in New York and New Guinea
Tobias Schneebaum

Outbound: Finding a Man, Sailing an Ocean
William Storandt

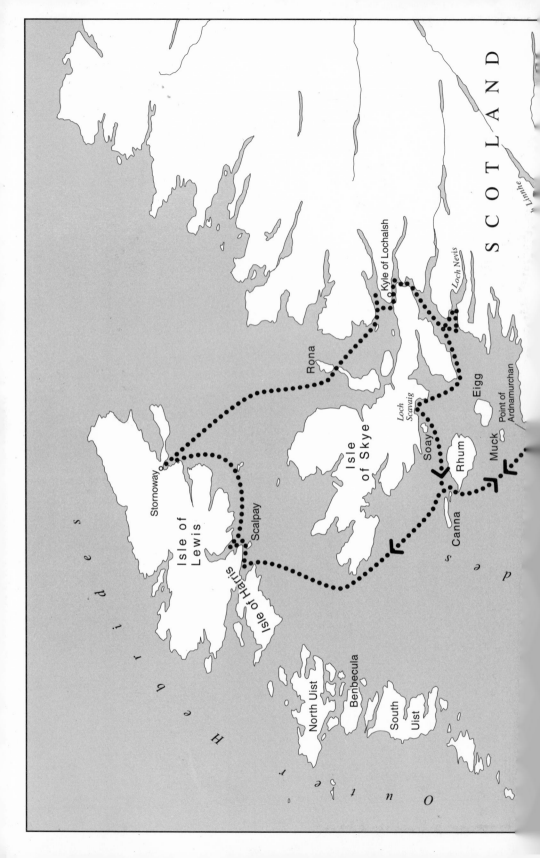